To Janie
with love & ———
       from

Grammummie

       March 21st, 1981

THE LIFE OF JESUS OF NAZARETH

EIGHTY·PICTURES
BY
WILLIAM·HOLE·
R·S·A : R·E

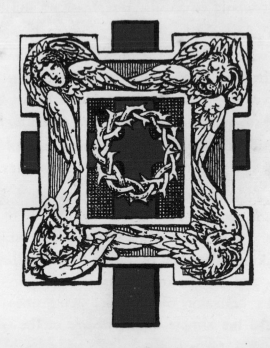

EYRE & SPOTTISWOODE
(BIBLE WAREHOUSE) LTD
LONDON

PREFATORY NOTE.

IN the backwaters of civilization, where the current of time flows past, leaving the manners and customs of a people unchanged, it is possible so to re-create the past, that pictures representing it may lay claim to a certain amount of historic accuracy. And thus it is in the land of Palestine, where observation of the primitive life of its inhabitants impresses the conviction that, in this respect at least, nothing of importance has been changed; but that as it was in the days of Jesus Christ, so it is to-day. Under such conditions, it is easier therefore to give a fairly truthful presentment of the country as it was two thousand years ago, than it would be to visualise the England of Elizabeth.

In these pictures I have aimed at the realization of nothing more than was visible to the outward eye of a contemporary, assuming the attitude of a follower of the prophet of Nazareth, who observed and recorded the incidents of his daily life, his mighty works and no less marvellous teaching, but with that dull perception of the profound significance of these things which was shared even by his chosen disciples.

Having adopted this standpoint with regard to the pictures themselves, it seems necessary to maintain it in the selection of a title for the work, and also in the following explanatory notes, speaking therefore of our Lord as "Jesus," not as "Christ"; and in referring to the Blessed Virgin and to the Apostles, by omission of the customary titles of reverence, using instead the simple nomenclature of the Gospels.

W. H.

PREFACE

ALTHOUGH, through the increased opportunities of travel, a growing number of persons from this country make the journey to Palestine, yet the expense must necessarily restrict these to a comparatively small number of the whole community. It is therefore an immense advantage to find placed in our hands the beautiful drawings of a skilled artist made on the spot in that country, to illustrate that Life which transcends in intensity of interest the biographies of even the greatest of men. Atmosphere, scenery, colour, architecture, costume, can all be revived by attentive study; reverent and sympathetic imagination, inspired by the Gospels and by the country, can achieve most of the rest.

Those who have not seen the Holy Land can have, without the assistance of such faithful pictorial rendering, very little idea of its beauty. It is a beauty in the first place of colour. The sun, it has been said, is the true magician in that country. To speak generally, it shines with brilliance during ten months of the year; the rain comes during two months, usually in November and February. The rainfall is about 23 inches, and is enough, if properly stored, to fertilize the greater part of the country throughout the year. No doubt in the days of the ancient civilization it was so stored; wherever now there is a pool or fountain or stream gushing from the limestone, the verdure is conspicuously rich. No doubt, also, the valleys and hillsides, except in country absolutely desert, like the Wilderness of Judæa in the south, were well supplied with trees.

Besides the fruit trees, olives, figs, citrons, quinces, almonds, pomegranates, and vines, there were oaks, ilexes, cedars, planes, firs, palms, fig-mulberries, and tree-oleanders. Much of the country is now denuded of forest, as the Turkish habit is to cut down and not re-plant; but there are pleasant woods on Carmel and Tabor, around Cæsarea Philippi, and the slopes of Hermon, on the hills and in the valleys of Galilee and Samaria, down the long course of the Jordan valley, about the Plain of Sharon, and in the country round Bethlehem. The mountain outlines, without being grand, are highly picturesque. The gleaming, snow-clad cone of Mount Hermon in the north is visible from every height through nearly the whole country. It is a land of mountains and hills, with few level spaces; the great Plain of Esdraelon, between the hills of Galilee and Samaria, the Plain of Sharon by the Mediterranean, and the deep gorge of Jordan are the chief. Carmel is a fine long ridge, with a bold head toward the sea; Gilboa has the look of pride which one expects in a mountain, with its group of well-defined peaks, and so has its neighbour, the Lesser Mount Hermon; Tabor has a commanding appearance from its lofty and isolated cone; Ebal and Gerizim are a noble pair of massive giants; and in Judæa there is the strange sight of mountains descending lower and lower, range after range, at decreasing levels, till they reach the depth of the Dead Sea Valley, 4,000 feet below Jerusalem, 1,300 feet below the Mediterranean. The deep depression of the Jordan valley runs through the whole length of the country, and draws into it the eastern sides of the central mountain ridges. From most of the hill-tops can be seen the blue line of the Mediterranean; and eastwards, beyond the Jordan, the whole of Palestine is dominated by the vast wall of the mountains of Bashan, Moab, and Edom, one huge chain of ramparts rearing themselves to an almost uniform level, and tinted with marvellous hues of pink, cobalt, purple, red, and gold. Features that must not be forgotten are the Lake of Gennesaret, the gem of the north; the beautiful River Jordan, deep, swift, sweet, and strong, fringed with innumerable flowering trees, where a multitude of birds sing morning and evening; and the 46 miles of the shining waters of the Dead Sea, reflecting every colour from the mountains on either side. Among the chief beauties of Palestine are the rich and varied flowers and plants: seringa, gladiolus, hollyhock, scarlet, blue, and white anemones in countless profusion, large varieties of lilies, cistus, mallow, larkspur, iris, narcissus, cyclamen, violet, rose, vetch, marigold, and genista, besides myrtle, box, balm, and bay. In the spring the hillsides are glorious with these in great profusion, especially in the north. One more source of beauty must be mentioned—the springs, fountains, and streams, such as those in Galilee, or in the fruit-gardens of En-gannim, or about the city of Samaria, or in Shechem (Nablûs), where water runs in all directions, and is guided into irrigation channels and beds with wonderfully rapid and repeated vegetable results, or the beautiful valley of Succoth, the tract of country which Jacob bought, or the Fountain of Elisha at Jericho, which scatters richness through the salt desert, or the lovely valley of the Jordan, with its tropical fruits and flowers. And over all these elements of the picturesque, and through all this fresh, keen, mountain air, the glorious sun, unchecked from dawn till sunset, weaves a brilliant charm of varied colours, bright to a degree to which Western eyes are unaccustomed, but subtle, mystic, blending one into another, and indescribably lovely. This impression is truly and faithfully conveyed by this delightful series.

The painter has been careful also in his study of costume, custom, and architecture. Many waves of fierce invasion and

B

oppressive conquest have swept over Palestine. It has been the battle-ground of Roman, Greek, Arabian, Crusader, Egyptian, Turk, as well as the modern nations of the West; there have been massacres, displacements, transplantations; but the dress, habits, and buildings of the East change but little. The long, loose robe of the Syrian, white, or with stripes of light pink, blue, green, or yellow, the outer coat with loose sleeves, the turban or caftan bound round the head with a fillet, the sandals, the dark blue or brown cloth of the peasants, the ornaments of the women, the differences between the northern and the southern tribes; these are undisturbed by conquest or change. The boat that plies to-day on the Lake of Gennesaret, the simple plough that tills the soil, the rude yoke that keeps the oxen together, the white houses with their inner courts and windows away from sun and stranger, the little stone-domed roofs, the flat tops and branch coverings of the cottages of the peasants; these, again, are probably as they were in the days of our Lord, or the time of Abraham, or that early Hittite civilization on which light has been thrown by Egyptian discovery. No doubt the Roman occupation in the time of our Lord had introduced finer buildings, better roads, and a far greater degree of prosperity than can be seen; no doubt the buildings of Herod the Great at Jerusalem, Samaria, and Jericho were of a noble Greek type, and of the magnificence which Josephus describes, and which their remains, both at Samaria and Jericho, indicate; no doubt the Crusaders left their mark on the architecture of the towns. But Jerusalem, with its magnificent circuit of battlemented walls, gates, and towers, built four hundred years ago by Sultan Solyman, its vast temple area of 35 acres, surrounding one of the most beautiful buildings of the world, the Mosque of Omar, its castle, domes, and minarets, its busy streets and crowded markets, its garden suburbs and tall, dark cypresses, must have the same general appearance that it had centuries ago. It is emphatically a noble city, on a superb site, seated in queenly dignity on its broad hill 2,700 feet above the Mediterranean, the centre of interest alike to Christian, Mussulman, and Jew. Hebron and Jaffa have older features; but in Jerusalem the general characteristics of the East are strong, predominant, and permanent.

Such was the country in which our Lord's earthly life was passed. With regard to our source of information about its details, it is unreasonable to ask why so little is contributed by either Jews or Pagans. Josephus, the Jewish historian, was an apostate to his religion, to whom Vespasian was more of a Messiah than any national hero; he mentions John Baptist, but is purposely silent about Christ. Philo lived at Alexandria, and it is doubtful whether he ever heard of the short ministry which was to make so wonderful a change in the world. It must be remembered that our Lord's life was intentionally obscure, that its incidents were only known to a few followers besides the general observation of the people; and that the authorities of the Jewish nation, stubbornly tenacious of their perversions of the Divine teaching through Moses and the prophets, combined to do their utmost to extinguish a doctrine which, by giving the true spiritual interpretation of the law, threatened their own pretensions. As to Roman writers, the little that they say confirms the accounts of the Gospels. Tacitus tells us that the Founder of Christianity had been put to death in the reign of Tiberius by the Procurator, Pontius Pilate, and that His religion—which Tacitus, knowing it only by hostile hearsay, calls a "deadly superstition"—though crushed for a time, burst forth again, not only throughout Judæa, in which it sprang up, but even in Rome.

Tacitus believed the most foolish legends and calumnies about
the origin and early history, even of the Jews. His contemporary Suetonius shared the same distorted opinions: he
mentions the Christians merely as coming under the punishment of Nero, and confuses Christ with some Chrestus whom
he supposes to be actually living in Rome. The younger
Pliny, on the other hand, informs the Emperor Trajan that
the Christians lived lives admittedly innocent, since he was
unable to establish against them any accusation beyond that
of the belief which, like his sceptical, philosophical, and
supercilious contemporaries, he regarded as a perverse and
extravagant superstition. The same letter tells us that
nothing could shake the allegiance of Christians to Christ,
and that they were accustomed to meet early in the morning
to celebrate Him as God with hymns of praise, and to bind
themselves with an oath to do no evil thing. Later in the
second century the hostile pagan writer Lucian alludes to the
crucifixion of Christ, to His miracles, to the mutual love and
help which prevailed among His followers, and their belief in
Him as Divine. Towards the close of the second century,
Celsus, the Platonist, whom we only know through the
writings of Origen, gives indisputable evidence that in his day
the facts of the Gospels, from first to last, were current in
the exact form in which we now possess them. "Thus,
from the scanty notices of heathens even, we can derive a
confirmation of the main external facts in the life of Christ:
His miracles, His parables, His crucifixion, His claim to
Divine honour, the devotion, innocence, heroic constancy and
mutual affection of His followers, and the progressive victories
won by His religion in spite of overwhelming opposition, alike
physical and intellectual."

The earliest written Christian evidence to the facts of the

life of Christ is that of the four Epistles of St. Paul, which
are practically undisputed: Galatians, Romans, Corinthians I.
and II. "It is the testimony of a man of commanding intellect,
and of the highest Jewish culture, who, after the death of
Christ, was converted from the most bitter hostility to the
most intense devotion, and who bears his witness within
twenty-five years of the events of which he spoke. And yet, if
we had the Epistles of St. Paul alone, we could find a contemporary testimony to almost every single fact of primary
importance in the life of Christ—His birth of the seed of
David, His poverty, His Messiahship, His moral teaching,
His proclamation of the Kingdom of God, His calling of the
apostles, His supernatural power, His divine claims, His
betrayal, His founding of the Last Supper, His passion, crucifixion, burial, resurrection, and repeated appearances." If we
add the evidence of the other Epistles, we have further
testimonies to almost every fact of importance in the Gospels,
as we have also in the General Epistles, and in the Revelation
of St. John."

What are the Gospels? The imagination of modern
criticism is trying to make out that the three earlier ones
are copies of a lost document, with amplifications according
to the taste and judgment of each writer. They certainly have
a large common element, but that itself again has great verbal
variations. It seems most probable that this large common
element in them represents the oral teaching of the apostles
when they lived together in Palestine, and which was repeated
Sunday by Sunday from memory in portions in the different
churches. At a later stage "an early tradition, circulated
perhaps in various churches, in Antioch, in Rome, in Ephesus,
in Corinth, before being embodied in a document, will naturally
have been modified and supplemented. . . . One version

will lay greater stress on the details of miracles; another on
the relations between Jesus and John the Baptist; another on
the law; another on the forgiveness of sins: and this varying
emphasis will produce modifications" (Dr. Abbot). Thus each
of the first three Evangelists, when beginning to commit to
paper what they remembered of the common oral tradition,
would have (under the guidance of the Divine Spirit) a special
store of his own, a special bent and predilection for his own
direction. The earliest literary tradition on the subject, that of
Papias, who wrote about 130–140 A.D., may not be worth
very much, but it points in the same line: "Mark was the
interpreter (translator or transcriber) of Peter. . . . Matthew
wrote his Scriptures in Hebrew, and each man interpreted
(translated or transcribed) them as best he could. . . . Mark,
having become Paul's interpreter, wrote down accurately all
that he remembered—not, however, in order—both the words
and deeds of Christ. For he neither heard our Lord, nor
attached himself to Him, but later on, as I said, attached
himself to Peter; who used to adapt his lessons to the needs
of the occasion, but not as though he were composing a
connected treatise of the discourses of the Lord; so that Mark
committed no error in writing down some matters just as he
remembered them. For one object was in his thoughts—to
make no omissions and no false statements in what he heard."
St. Luke is referred to by name as the author of the third
Gospel by Irenaeus, and in the remarkable fragment called the
Muratorian Canon (A.D. 170). The same document speaks of
the authorship of the fourth Gospel. It is obviously an
account handed down from old days. It is there said that
"being requested by his fellow-disciples and bishops to write,
John desired them to fast for three days, and then to relate to
one another what revelation each had received either for or

against the project. The same night it was revealed to Andrew that while all called the past to mind, John should write in his own name." Recent discoveries and investigations have made it certain that all four Gospels were current before the middle of the second century. Justin Martyr (who wrote about 145–147 A.D.) says that in his day the Memoirs of the Apostles were read with the Books of the Prophets in the service of the Church. At a date little later than this a Harmony of these appears to have been published under the name of Diatessaron, or fourfold Gospel, by Tatian, a disciple of Justin Martyr. About this time the Gospels seem to have been translated into Latin, soon afterwards into Syriac, and then into the Egyptian dialects. By the end of the century they occupy a position very similar to that which we now describe as "Canonical."

The artist accepts the authenticity and authority of the four Gospels, according to the general consent and belief of the whole Church of Christ. The strongest evidence for the truth of the Gospel history is to be found in the Gospels themselves. It is impossible to separate the miraculous from the non-miraculous portions, even if it were possible to explain Christianity without miracles. The narrative, taken as it stands, forms a consistent and coherent whole, and explain the facts so as nothing else can explain them. The claim to judge the life of Christ as a dry scientific document, without allowing for the preliminary fact of His divine nature, and its consequent results in supernatural influence on the things and persons that surround Him, is surely contrary to the principles of History, Science, and Reason. The facts of Christianity can be accounted for in no other way than by taking account of the great underlying hypothesis : to leave that hypothesis out in the supposed interests of History and Science, is to destroy the possibility of arriving at a true historical and scientific conclusion. Of miracles in general it has been well said by Farrar in his "Life of Christ": "If we once understand that the word Nature has little or no meaning unless it be made to include the idea of its Author; if we once realize the fact, which all science teaches us, that the simplest and most elementary operation of the Laws of Nature is infinitely beyond the comprehension of our most exalted intelligence; if we once believe that the Divine Providence of God is no far-off abstraction, but a living and loving care over the lives of men; lastly, if we once believe that Christ was the only-begotten Son of God, the Word of God Who came to reveal and declare His Father to mankind; then there is nothing in any Gospel miracle to shock our faith. We shall regard the miracles of Christ as resulting from the fact of His Being and His mission, no less naturally and inevitably than that the rays of light stream outwards from the sun. They were, to use the favourite expression of St. John, not mere 'portents' or 'powers,' or 'signs,' but they were 'works'— the ordinary and inevitable works whenever He chose to exercise them, of One Whose very existence was the highest miracle of all. For our faith is that He was sinless . . . the fulfilment of the Moral Law . . . That fulfilment makes us believe that He was indeed Divine; and if He were Divine, we have no further astonishment left when we are taught that He did on earth that which can be done by the Power of God alone."

The Life of our Lord may be divided into Five Epochs:—

    I. The Infancy and Childhood. (Pictures 1–10.)

    II. The Youth and Early Manhood. (Pictures 11, 12.)

III. The Public Ministry:—

    1. The Early Scenes in St. John's Gospel. (Pictures 13–22.)

    2. The Galilæan Ministry till the murder of the Baptist. (Pictures 23–40.)

    3. The period of decided opposition.

    4. The period of departure and peril until the final farewell to Galilee. (Pictures 41–44.)

    5. From the great journey to Jerusalem till the retirement to Ephraim beyond Jordan. (Pictures 45–49.)

    6. From this retirement to the Passover. (Pictures 50–54.)

IV. The Closing Scenes and Crucifixion. (Pictures 55–71.)

V. The Resurrection and Ascension. (Pictures 72–80.)

Of the Infancy and Childhood only four or five events are related to us: two by St. Matthew, and three by St. Luke. Our Lord chose that His early life should be unnoticed: it was His public work and teaching that was to be of transcendent importance. Each of the five early exceptions has a distinct purpose: the Vision of the Shepherds is to assure us that Heaven was watching the momentous Birth; the Circumcision is to record that he was born under the Law, to fulfil it; the Presentation in the Temple, thirty-three days after the Circumcision, while the family were still staying at Bethlehem, is to remind us that there were those who, like Simeon and Anna, were waiting for the fulfilment of prophecy; the Visit of the Wise Men from the East is to suggest the homage of ancient Eastern faiths; the Massacre of the Children at Bethlehem, and the Flight into Egypt, are to prepare the mind for the suffering and rejection that were

c

inseparable from the appearance of the True Light in a sinful, darkened, and alienated world. The reason why some incidents relating to the Incarnation are mentioned by St. Matthew and others by St. Luke, is not far to seek. St. Matthew gives his episodes on the authority of Joseph, and they are such as Joseph would be likely to mention; St. Luke's are those which were better known to the mother herself, and are clearly related on her authority, or that of her intimate friends. St. Mark, handing down the practical teaching of St. Peter, begins at once with the Ministry; of the Birth and early years he had no personal knowledge, and they would not be likely to enter so much into the exhortations of his teacher. St. John is said to have read the three earlier Gospels, and to have praised them highly as far as they went, but thought they needed supplementing; accordingly he had no need to repeat the accounts of the Infancy, but begins with his sublime theological meditation on the Eternal Word, which he merges into the mission of the Baptist.

I propose to offer a few notes on the ten pictures belonging to the period of the Infancy and Childhood, and then to pass on to the other sections. No. 1 brings us face to face with the problem of angelic appearances. If we believe, with the whole Christian Church, that Christ was a Revelation of the Divine, then it would be strange if no other glimpses into supernatural and spiritual life should have accompanied His manifestation. It is impossible to suppose that the spiritual world is untenanted except by the Divine Being, and the souls belonging to this minute globe: that there are heavenly hosts of incalculable multitudes and innumerable degrees is what we should expect. Of spiritual forms we can frame not even the remotest conception : but when, on due occasions, spiritual messengers from the spiritual world were allowed to shine through the veil of time and space, it would be reasonable that they should appear, not in some strange and unintelligible mystery, but in a vision corresponding to human capacity to see and understand. This is the idea of the painter : his treatment of angelic appearance is supernatural, spiritual, mysterious, suggestive, yet following the limits of human experience. No. 2 presents another rule by which the painter has given vitality to his drawings : the costumes are not imaginary, but taken from different parts of Palestine. Here Mary, from Nazareth, wears the dress of the north : Elisabeth, from the neighbourhood of Hebron, that of the south. No. 3 should bring home vividly to those who see it the different conditions between the life of our experience and that of the East, of which the total publicity of the inn is one of the most noticeable. In No. 4 the question suggests itself why was the announcement of the moment of the Incarnation made to the shepherds ? Their occupation was one of the humblest in the estimation of the Jews. It was partly probably because the heavenly choir must signalize such an event in any case within the ken of the earth and its inhabitants, whether any were there to hear or not; partly because the shepherds, or some of them, were necessarily awake to guard their flocks from robbers and beasts of prey; and partly also because the message which the Son of God was to deliver was to concern even the very poorest and meanest of mankind. In No. 5 we remember that Justin Martyr and the earliest tradition maintained that the Birth took place in a cave; that St. Jerome handed down the evidence of old people that the Church of Bethlehem was on the site of the ruined inn : that this site is on the edge of the rocky eminence on which Bethlehem is built ; and

that when Joseph and Mary found no room in the courtyard,
which was the main part of the inn, or in the covered recess
where travellers placed their mattresses, they would be glad to
go aside to some hollowed recess in the side of the hill,
such as is not uncommon at the inns of so mountainous a
country as Palestine, which was used as an adjunct where
extra animals could be tethered.   In No. 6 the architecture is
a reminder that Herod the Great had lately rebuilt the Temple
at Jerusalem on a very magnificent scale, ample details of
which are given us by Josephus.   This was mainly in the
Greek style, but it would have some admixtures of Eastern
taste—reminiscences of the former Temples.   The Roman
guard in No. 7 suggests the foreign occupation, the busy
people, the changeless life of the cities and bazaars of the
East; and the three wise men representing the cultures of
Persia, India, and China, are in harmony with that insatiable
thirst for knowledge which made such men travel to Athens
and Rome, and other centres in its pursuit.   In No. 8 the
characteristics of the three religions are faithfully produced:
and the family is shown to have settled for a time in a fitting
and simple apartment such as at this day would be found in
Bethlehem.   The stay in Egypt (No. 9) was probably not
long as Herod soon died, to be succeeded by Archelaus.   The
border of Egypt was not much more than 100 miles from
Bethlehem, about the same distance as Nazareth in the north.
Egypt was the common asylum for distressed inhabitants of
Palestine, from the times of Abraham and Jeroboam, and
Jeremiah.   The massacre of a score or two of children in
Bethlehem was too small an item in the record of Herod's
cruelties to be chronicled by Josephus, though it seems to be
alluded to by a later writer, Macrobius: "On Augustus being
informed that among the boys under two years of age, whom

Herod ordered to be slain in Syria, his own son also had been slain, 'It is better,' said he, 'to be Herod's pig than his son.'" "Herod had massacred priests and nobles; he had decimated the Sanhedrin; he had caused the High Priest, his brother-in-law, the young and noble Aristobulus, to be drowned in pretended sport before his eyes; he had ordered the strangulation of his favourite wife, the beautiful Mariamne. His sons Alexander, Aristobulus, and Antipater: his uncle Joseph—Antigones and Alexander, the uncle and father of his wife,—his mother-in-law, Alexandra—his kinsman, Costobaras—his friends, Dositheus and Gadias, were but a few of the multitudes of his victims . . . Deaths by strangulation, by burning, by being cleft asunder, by secret assassination, confessions forced by unutterable torture . . . mark the annals of a reign that was so cruel that, in the energetic language of the Jewish ambassadors to the Emperor Augustus, 'The survivors during his life-time were even more miserable than the sufferers.'" No. 10 gives an admirable realization of Nazareth, with Mary and her little Son in the foreground. In the well itself, the painter has followed the outlines of the arch left by the Crusaders, but with an earlier style. The women and children of Nazareth are distinguished to-day by their brightness and attractive looks. The habit of carrying water-jars and other burdens on the head gives all the women of Palestine a notably graceful carriage.

II.—Of the Youth and Early Manhood so little is said, that we have only two pictures—Jesus among the Doctors, and Jesus at Home at Nazareth. Although we should have wished with all our hearts to know some of the things that were said and done during those long silent years at Nazareth, it is important that we should not know them. What we have to know about our Lord is His example and His teaching;

and He did not begin to teach till His public ministry. "Jesus increased in wisdom as in stature." The quiet years at Nazareth were a preparation: if we knew more about them they might call attention away from the ministry. Our attitude must be like that of St. Paul: "Yea, though we have known Christ after the flesh, yet now henceforth know we him (so) no more." The visit to the Temple (No. 11) has been sometimes mistaken. Jesus did not go to impress the Rabbis with His insight into the Law, but to hear the theological lectures delivered by them to the young men of Jerusalem in one of the schools of the Temple adjoining the court of the Gentiles. Here His questions and answers were natural and appropriate. No. 12 illustrates in a most beautiful and touching manner the fact alluded to in the question in St. Mark vi. 3: "Is not this the carpenter?" To all the sons of manual toil it is an inspiration and encouragement to realize that the Son of God as Man laboured with His hands.

III.—*The Public Ministry. Section 1 contains, to speak generally, the supplementary scenes supplied in the early part of St. John's Gospel* (Pictures 13–22). Our Lord received Baptism (No. 13) as ratifying the mission of His great forerunner—the last and greatest child of the Old Dispensation, the earliest herald of the New; and He also received it as the beautiful symbol of moral purification, and the humble inauguration of a ministry which "came not to destroy the Law but to fulfil." By receiving it He consecrated the Sacrament of Entrance into His Kingdom. In the descent of the Spirit, the resemblance to the dove should not be exaggerated. Three of the Evangelists (St. Matthew, St. Mark, and St. Luke) say that the Baptist saw the Spirit descending like a dove, an undulating glory like the gentle flight and wings of a dove: "From the cleft heavens streamed the Spirit of God in a dove-like radiance that seemed to hover over His head in lambent flame." The exaggeration has come through misunderstanding St. Luke's version of this phraseology: he speaks of the vision coming in a bodily shape like a dove; not meaning more than the others, but only insisting that the spiritual glory had a distinct entity. No. 14. The traditional scene of the Temptation is the side of the mountain west of Jericho called Quarantania (that of the Forty Days), the last rampart of the descending ranges of the Wilderness of Judæa towards the Plain of the Dead Sea. The subject of the Temptation at this crisis was obviously the methods to be adopted in the ministry. No. 15. The independence of the Evangelists of each other is illustrated by the fact that the order of the Temptation is different in St. Matthew and St. Luke. No. 16. "All the kingdoms of the world in a moment of time" (St. Luke iv. 5), certainly implies a vision, and not an actual sight. No indication of where the exceeding high mountain was, is given: but the painter is fully warranted in making it snow-capped, and giving it an air of mystery. In No. 17 we have the earlier call of John, Andrew, Simon, and James; in No. 18 the addition of Philip and Nathanael. In this the painter has given a glimpse of one of the most beautiful parts of the main road from south to north through Palestine. No. 19. Cana is a few miles north-east of Nazareth on the way to the Lake of Gennesaret. The house chosen for the scene is characteristic of the better-class Syrian family. A boy is pouring the last of the wine into a jug: the water-carrier has come to replenish the jars: servants are carrying fresh dishes to the large upper room. No. 20. The Temple area covers 35 acres; the outer courts in Herod's building must have been very spacious and handsome. Our Lord is seen causing the evacuation by the simple majesty of His moral authority. It need excite no surprise that the act was

repeated after an interval of three years: where gain is con-
cerned, and the authorities are corrupt and on the side of
malpractices, such evils are absolutely sure of recrudescence.
No. 21 gives a vivid impression of Jerusalem at night in the
present day: the distant Mount of Olives, the brilliant stars,
the twinkling lights, the uneven levels of the city, the flat
roofs with their little domes, the opportunity for outdoor life.
It would have been strange if a few of the less prejudiced of
the rulers had not been attracted by the lofty spirituality and
deep insight of our Lord's teaching. No. 22. Jacob's Well is
near the village of Ischar, a short distance south of Shechem
(Nablûs), and below the slopes of Mount Gerizim. There is
a descent from a level of the ground down to the well by an
architectural staircase and covering, now in ruins.

We now come to the *Second Section of Part III., The Galilæan Ministries till the Murder of the Baptist.* (Pictures 23–40.)

Up till now our Lord's work had been preparatory. With
the Sermon in the Synagogue at Nazareth (No. 23) a new
epoch begins. The interior in the picture is taken from the
oldest synagogue in Jerusalem, that of the Sephardim Jews,
with the rostrum for the elders, the lectern for the reader, the
receptacle for the Manuscripts, &c. The rejection at Nazareth
was exceedingly likely to happen, as the simple peasants were
unprepared for authoritative teaching from one whom they
had known as one of themselves. No. 24. Capernaum, which
our Lord chose as His home after leaving Nazareth, was a
prosperous little city by the north-west shore of the Lake of
Gennesaret, on the Roman road that ran through the north
of Palestine, and now a tract of country of extraordinary
fertility. The street in Jaffa gives a fair idea of the interior
of a Syrian town. It is a happy touch of the painter that he
has shown our Lord as paying attention first to a sick child.

No. 25. The Lake of Gennesaret is 682 feet below the level
of the Mediterranean, and its climate and produce are tropical.
Palms, oleanders, bananas, and many kinds of fruit-trees
flourish. It is surrounded with hills, which are divided by
clefts and gorges. The villages and towns were mostly on the
north and west, as the eastern shores are nearly precipitous.
From the colours of the hills, the brilliance of sky and
water, the many-hued atmosphere, and the richness of vegetation, the Lake has a smiling charm of its own, which would
make it attractive even without its sacred associations. This
must have been greatly enhanced in the time of our Lord by
the well-built towns, the Greek architecture, the busy com-
mercial life, the numerous boats skimming here and there from
port to port. Two merchants in the picture illustrate the
cares of this life, two idle boys the stony ground. No. 26.
Each of our Lord's miracles had its own special meaning and
teaching. The draught of fishes was exactly suited to impress
Simon Peter and his companions, and to fit them for the
second call—that to become fishers of men. No. 27. Still at
Capernaum, we see the Water-gate of the town, where Matthew
would be employed, with others, in levying custom on goods
brought in. "These imposts were to the Jews pre-eminently
distasteful. The mere fact of having to pay them wounded
their tenderest sensibilities. They were not only a badge of
servitude; they were not only a daily sign that God seemed
to have forsaken His land, and that all the splendid Messianic
hopes of their earlier history were merged in the disastrous
twilight of subjugation to a foreign rule; but more than this,
the payment of such imposts wore almost the appearance of
apostacy to the sensitive and scrupulous mind of a genuine
Jew. It seemed to be a violation of the first principles of the
Theocracy, such as could only be excused as the result of

D

absolute compulsion." No. 28. Early in His Galilæan ministry our Lord gave the outline of His moral teaching, first to
the inner circle of disciples and then to the gathered crowd.
It was on a mountain, so that there might be no interruption.
No site could possibly be more suitable than the mountain
known as the Horns of Hattin. It is on the road from
Nazareth and Cana to the towns of the Lake; it is near the
Lake, and commands an enchanting view of its whole surface
and surroundings. On the top is a grassy plain of a few
acres, with a high group of rocks at each end, from either of
which, in that clear air, the voice could be heard by several
thousands of people. Of the momentous effect of the Sermon
on the Mount in the history of the world it is unnecessary to
speak. No. 29. Just such a village, but now a ruinous heap
of mud huts, exists at the foot of Kurn Hattin. Leprosy,
from its degrading loathsomeness, and its analogy to sin,
always aroused the strongest compassion from our Lord.
No. 30. Of great numbers of our Lord's works either no
mention is made or no details given. The healing of the
centurion's servant of the palsy is mentioned at length, partly
because it brings Christ in connection with the Roman world,
partly because of the conspicuous faith of the man himself.
No. 31. Nain ("The Fair") is in a beautiful situation on
the slopes of Lesser Mount Hermon, near Endor, opposite
Nazareth, about ten miles to the south, across the Plain of
Esdraelon. It is quite likely that our Lord was acquainted
with the widow and her son. At any rate, the circumstances
were so touching that He thought it a fit occasion to exert
His greatest power, as He is only recorded to have done on
two other occasions: for the little daughter of the excellent
ruler of the synagogue of Capernaum, and for His friends
Martha and Mary, in the case of their brother. No. 32. The

incident of the devotion of the sinful woman in the house of Simon the Pharisee is well selected for illustration, as it shows our Lord's divine power alike in attracting and reforming. No. 33. "This is a stupendous miracle, one of those which test whether we indeed believe in the credibility of the miraculous or not; one of those miracles of power which cannot be explained away by existing laws . . . If we believe that God rules: if we believe that Christ rose: if we have reason to hold, among the deepest convictions of our being, the certainty that God has not delegated His sovereignty or His providence to the final, unintelligent, pitiless, inevitable working of material forces: if we see on every page of the Evangelists the quiet simplicity of truthful and faithful witnesses: if we see in every year of succeeding history, in every experience of individual life, a confirmation of the testimony which they delivered—then we shall neither clutch at rationalistic interpretations, nor be much troubled if others adopt them. He who believes, he who knows, the efficacy of prayer, in what other men may regard as the inevitable certainties or blindly-directed accidents of life—he who has felt how the voice of a Saviour, heard across the long generations, can calm wilder storms than ever buffeted into fury the bosom of the inland Lake—he who sees in the Person of his Redeemer a fact more stupendous and more majestic than all these observed sequences which men endow with an imaginary omnipotence, and worship under the name of Law—to him at least there will be neither difficulty nor hesitation in supposing that Christ, on board that half-wrecked fishing-boat, did utter His mandate, and that the wind and the sea obeyed; that HIS WORD was indeed more potent among the cosmic forces than miles of agitated water, or leagues of rushing air" (Farrar). No. 34. Possession by evil spirits is now represented by various forms of mental malady verging towards lunacy, and by the different phases of epilepsy and kindred diseases. The morning light on the Lake in this picture is exquisitely rendered. No. 35. In Northern Palestine the roofs of the inferior houses are made of a few beams, which support a layer of boughs of trees; on the top of these are leaves and branches, and the whole is sometimes covered with a light layer of earth and grass. A hole in the roof, therefore, is very easily made. In this picture the roof is in the foreground; the healing has just taken place within: some of the crowd stand outside in the street below: the Lake and a more substantial house are in the background. No. 36. The healing of the woman who touched the hem of Christ's garment in the crowd has always been an inspiration and encouragement to Christians in doubt and difficulty. The street scene is partly adapted from Jerusalem. No. 37. When, to the parents of Jairus' little daughter, He added His customary warning that they should not speak of what had happened, it was not with the intention that the entire fact should remain unknown—for that would have been impossible—but because those who have received from God's hand unbounded mercy are more likely to reverence that mercy with adoring gratitude, if it be kept like a hidden treasure in the inmost heart. No. 38. The words about the angel stirring the pool are a gloss, and not in the best MSS. It was an intermittent medicinal spring; the Bath at Tiberias—from which this sketch is taken—is of the same character. No. 39. In the miracle of feeding the multitude, twice enacted, the processes of nature, which extend over a year, were concentrated into a few moments by the Divine Power in which nature exists. No. 40. The same comment, given on the Stilling of the Tempest (No. 33), applies to the Walking on the Water.

Part III (3).—*The Period of Decided Opposition.* On this part of our Lord's life no illustrations happen to be given. The machinations of the Priests, Pharisees, and Scribes from Jerusalem were now influencing the people in Galilee, who were themselves disappointed that Christ would not be made a king.

Part III (4).—*The Period of Departure and Peril, until the Final Farewell to Galilee.* (Pictures 41–46.)

No. 41. This retirement from His own country brought Him into the interesting coast districts that extend from Carmel to Beyrout, including Acre, Tyre, Zarephath, Sidon, &c., the land of the Phoenicians. The object of Christ's delay in granting the petitioner's wish is partly to prove her faith, partly to emphasize the greatness of the move in including Gentiles in the scope of His Ministry. No. 42. It was during this period of absence, when they were in the neighbourhood of Cæsarea Philippi, that our Lord asked His disciples their opinion about His Mission. It is a beautiful region of hill-slopes, cool green woods, and abundant streams. No. 43. The Transfiguration, or temporary glorification of the Son of Man, with the Vision of Moses (the representation of the Law), and Elijah (the representative of the Prophets), was granted at this time to deepen the Apostles' faith, and to show the close relation between His revelation and their teaching. It could not have taken place on Mount Tabor, as that was then crowned by a Roman garrison; the slopes of Mount Hermon, in the region of Cæsarea Philippi, are far more likely. No. 44. This miracle is doubtless specially recorded in order to lay stress on our Lord's words: "This kind cometh not out but by prayer and fasting": meaning that for higher spiritual effects and deeper moral influence, special devotion, earnestness, purpose and seriousness are necessary. A flippant life is a poor exponent of sentiments, however in themselves exalted. No. 45. It is difficult to say exactly in what part of our Lord's life the incident of the woman in the Temple took place: St. John implies that our Lord made several visits to Jerusalem, and the distances in Palestine are so short that there might have been several such not specially recorded. The incident, though apparently not in the original MS. of St. John's Gospel, is so entirely in harmony with His character and teaching that its presence in the text is welcomed as of equal authority with the rest. No. 46. The ingratitude of the nine lepers no doubt added to our Lord's sorrow just now at the growing influence of the opposition of His enemies.

Part III (5).—*From the Great Journey to Jerusalem till the Retirement to Ephraim beyond Jordan.* (Pictures 47–49.)

No. 47. In the middle of the little village of Bethany, two miles S.E. from Jerusalem, round a great shoulder of the Mount of Olives, are the ruins of an important house. Here some years ago a French explorer discovered in the base the remains of an ancient chapel. This seems to point with strong probability to a valid tradition of the site of the house of Martha, Mary, and Lazarus. No. 48. The blessing of the little children took place in some town on the east side of Jordan, during His retirement to that part of Ephraim that was across the river. That kindly and gentle act has been of incalculable consequence to the life of children in the subsequent development of Christian civilization. No. 49. St. John tells us that our Lord set out for the raising of Lazarus from the place where He was staying beyond Jordan. It should be noticed again that the three cases of recall from the dead were where our Lord's own sympathies were strongly aroused.

Part III (6).—*From the Retirement beyond Jordan to the Passover.* (Pictures 50–54.)

No. 50. The summoning of Zacchæus to entertain our Lord at Jericho was amongst the most remarkable of the closing acts of our Lord's Ministry. Jericho was a somewhat fashionable town, rebuilt by Herod at the débouchure of the steep road down from Jerusalem to the Plain. To signalize the despised tax-gatherer in such a way was to teach a permanent lesson of absolute unworldliness. No. 51. The entirely separate independence of the Evangelists is again shown by the fact that St. Matthew mentions two blind men on this occasion, St. Mark only Bartimæus. Bartimæus was obviously the best known of the two. No. 52. Our Lord, for the confirmation of the faith of His followers, took opportunities as they occurred for the fulfilment of Prophecy. The triumphal entry into Jerusalem was one of these. At the same time it was once more an impressive lesson of unworldliness, and of the purely spiritual nature of His Kingdom. The painter has emphasized this by introducing an incident that might easily have happened: the Roman Governor, Pontius Pilate, being carried by with the significant emblem of earthly power. No. 53. The final determination of the priests to bring matters to a climax is powerfully expressed in this picture. No. 54. This incident in our Lord's last days has been little noticed. The Mount of Olives still deserves its name, but in the flourishing days of the Herodian kingdom and the Roman influence, before Titus had cut down all the trees round the city, and when there was no Turkish misrule to discourage the cultivation of trees, it must have been a pleasant and shady retreat. It is a little higher than Mount Zion, but generally on a level with it, with the deep valley of the Kedron between. The course of that stream was 120 feet lower at that time

than it is at present. Jerusalem, in all its beauty and majesty,
lies opposite, crowning the hill—a mass of battlemented walls,
towers, gateways, and fair buildings. Among the trees, on
Olivet, after long days of teaching and argument, our Lord
would find rest, meditation, and strength for the awful conflict
that was to come. It is little touches such as this that bring
home the truthfulness, the simplicity, the coherence, the overwhelming force of the whole Gospel history.

Part IV.—*The Closing Scenes and Crucifixion.* (Pictures
55–71.)

No. 55. The washing of the disciples' feet as they lay,
after the prevalent custom, at supper, was a final lesson of
unworldliness, humility, and readiness to perform even the
humblest tasks in the Divine cause of the service of man.
In the East, in the heat and dust, and where sandals are worn,
the washing of the feet is a necessary and refreshing usage,
ordinarily performed by slaves. No. 56. The look of anguish
and tragedy is already on the Master's face. This is one of
the most solemn and pathetic scenes of His life: the institution
of the pledge of His perpetual presence, His communication
of Divine grace, His union with His people, and their union
through Him with each other. Would that the sacred remembrance of Him had always been reverenced in its breadth
and depth, and been jealously guarded from all dispute and
excess of metaphysical investigation! No. 57. Gethsemane
means "The Oil-press." It was a garden, probably with an
inclosure, belonging to some proprietor who made oil of the
olives. It was a familiar resort to our Lord and His disciples,
and may well have been where tradition places it. The site
is owned by the Russians, who have turned it into a neat and
trim garden with walks and flower-beds amongst the ancient

trees, and a bright new white church on the upper level, with five large gilded bulbous domes. It is pleasant to turn from such a recollection to the solemn, sympathetic, and truthful imagery of the picture, where our Lord's human nature is, through deep tribulation, finally rising to the height of the Divine. No. 58. The glare of the lanterns and torches among the cool shadows of the moonlight glades is admirably represented. Some of the assailants have already stumbled backwards, awed by the simple inherent, incontestable majesty of the Son of Man who was the Son of God. No. 59. There were six examinations of our Lord: (1) before Annas for fact; (2) before Caiaphas, for determination; (3) before the Sanhedrin at dawn of day for official confirmation; (4) before Pilate for preliminary inquiry; (5) before Herod Antipas as Tetrarch of Galilee; (6) before Pilate for final acquittal or condemnation. This picture represents No. (3) in one of the council chambers of the Temple. No. 60. Our Lord, as He is being led away from the Council to the Palace of Pilate, turns and looks at Peter, as he is warming himself by a fire in the courtyard among the servants of Caiaphas. No. 61. The Jews would not go into the Judgment Hall, so Pilate met them in the portico of his house. It was the splendid palace built for himself by Herod the Great, fully described by Josephus, a marvel of Roman dignity and luxury. No. 62. Pilate takes the Accused into a room in the interior, converses with Him, and is determined if he possibly can to acquit Him, being absolutely convinced of His character and innocence. No. 63. Antipas, one of the most worthless of men, had come to Jerusalem for the gaieties of the Passover, and was probably occupying, with his ladies and retinue, the older Idumæan Palace. The Herods were devoted to hunting, and had special hunting grounds near the Lake of Gennesaret, particularly

E

near Bethsaida Julias, so a favourite hound is appropriately introduced. The dissolute prince is telling his ladies what he has heard of this wonderful Prisoner. No. 64. The painful scene of the scourging in the barrack-yard on a truncated pillar is depicted with vivid imagination. Two soldiers in half-dress are looking on from an entry: another is bringing in a sack of corn: a fourth is finishing the buckling of his accoutrements as he goes on guard. A servant is bringing in water, and a barrack-boy, with characteristic love of the horrible, is looking on with absorbed interest. No. 65. The barrack-room scene is also wonderfully lifelike: the attitudes of the brutal soldiers, the dregs of the provinces: the scrawling on the walls: the utter self-isolation and unconsciousness of our Lord of such surroundings. No. 66. Accusations to Rome had a meaning for Pilate, as his rule had been cruel, unjust, and turbulent. Very reluctantly he gave way to the persistent and threatening malignity of the leaders of the Jews and their satellites. No. 67. This is a true realization of the Via Dolorosa, a long narrow street running between the north boundary of the great Temple area and the Palace of Pilate. Fragments of the Roman pavement of the Prætorium have lately been discovered among the buildings on the left of the picture. No. 68. It will be impossible ever to discover finally and indisputably the scene of the Crucifixion. The traditional site, though now in the city, was certainly in the time of our Lord outside, as remains of the northern wall of that day have been discovered south of it. And Gordon's site, the Garden Tomb and Skull Hill, is rather far away, and selected for reasons that appeal more perhaps to imagination than to reason. Curiosity about such matters may easily be exaggerated: at any rate, the great Atonement took place within a certain area. No. 69. From the apprehension in the Garden till the moment of Crucifixion our Lord had had no opportunity of making provision for His mother. Now she is there, in her motherly place beside her Son's last agony, and with His dying breath He tenderly makes His arrangement for her. No. 70. The darkness, the earthquake, and above all the demeanour of our Lord on the Cross changed mockery to awe, and scorn to reverence. "The centurion and they that were with him feared greatly, saying, Truly this man was the Son of God." The spectators "smote their breasts, and returned." No. 71. The rich man, Joseph of Arimathæa, has the privilege of burial. His garden and tomb were close to the very spot of the Crucifixion. Nicodemus brought an immense weight of spices for the embalming.

Part V.—*The Resurrection and Ascension.* (Pictures 72–80.)

No. 72. The women bringing their own spices were naturally first at the tomb. Our Lord was not seen consecutively for long by any. His various appearances in His risen glory are recorded from different experiences and accounts by the four Evangelists and by St. Paul, and are perfectly harmonious. No. 73. Next came Peter and John, on the report of the women. No. 74. Mary Magdalene had lingered in the garden, in her great sorrow, love, and despair, and she who had loved much because much had been forgiven her was allowed the first sight of the Risen Lord. No. 75. The preparation of the two disciples by our Lord's discourse with them on the way to Emmaus, was a natural step towards the full belief of the whole number. No. 76. Before they could reach the Eleven, the Lord had appeared unto Simon; a special revelation of which the painter has made touching and forcible use in the picture. No. 77. The second appearance of our Lord to the company of His disciples is naturally chosen by the painter, as it introduces the striking pathetic and encouraging incident of St. Thomas.   No. 78. Our Lord had promised to meet His disciples again in the familiar haunts and associations of peaceful Galilee, and the beloved Lake, far from the harrowing recollections of the last days at Jerusalem: and St. John gives the details of the meeting. No. 79. The Ascension was clearly in the country near Bethany.   The painter has depicted the glimpse into the spiritual world, and the circling company of angelic beings, as the "Cloud of Light" received His spiritual human form, and He passed beyond the bounds of Time and Sense. No. 80. The beautiful thought of the last picture will appeal to every heart.   It is the interior of an early church in primitive days: Holy Communion is being celebrated in obedience to the Lord's dying commands: the lights are shining at the Sacred Feast, and above is seen the spiritual form of the Lord in blessing, and in fulfilment of His promise, of which the whole history of true Christian civilization is the fulfilment: "Lo, I am with you alway, even unto the end of the world!"

WILLIAM SINCLAIR,

Archdeacon of London.

INTRODUCTORY NOTE.

BY

Dr. GEORGE ADAM SMITH,

PROFESSOR OF OLD TESTAMENT LANGUAGE, LITERATURE AND THEOLOGY IN THE
UNITED FREE CHURCH COLLEGE, GLASGOW.
AUTHOR OF THE "HISTORICAL GEOGRAPHY OF THE HOLY LAND."

I HAVE been permitted to make a gradual study of these pictures of the earthly life of our Lord, and to receive from time to time, as they grew, the grace of their influence: a freshness born not of mere skill, but of truth and reverence. I am not competent to speak of their art; except as the common man may feel its truthfulness, its simplicity and its reserve. It is as a common man of the land and time in which his subjects happened, that the artist has drawn near to them—in the course of their happening, and before there had risen upon them that later light, which, while it reveals their full significance in the purpose of God, not only dazzles our eyes to the actual shapes of their happening but is apt to dispel the fresh, morning wonder of their entry into the world. The artist has striven to see and to show to us what in those great hours any one with a keen eye might have seen of earth and air, of flowers and stones, of the faces and figures of men, and of the motion of crowds, but with a wonder at his heart, which he was still unable, or forbore, to explain and define. For it is in art as in worship. There is a *standing afar off* to which the vision and the secret are given, as they are not to a confidence which presses in, is proud of understanding all, and becomes familiar.

Every one who knows the land and the atmosphere will feel them again in these pictures. The white glare of eastern day is where it should be—upon the road out of Jericho by which Bartimæus sat—for nowhere else does it beat more fiercely. But this is not (as some painters have imagined) the only or even the prevalent light of Palestine; and in the variety of their atmospheres the pictures are true to all that change of sky and stir of air, which returned pilgrims remember as even more characteristic of the land than its blazing sun. For instance:—in the Jordan Valley the gathered clouds and sudden rising of the wind before which the Solitary Figure is *driven of the Spirit into the wilderness,*[1] the lights and shadows under the trees, and on the rushing waters, of Banias;[2] the fresh hill-air about the village below the Mount of Transfiguration; the noontide sun upon Jacob's Well;[3] evening over Jerusalem from the Mount of Olives, with the red skies behind the terraced buildings, and the smoke of the evening sacrifice;[4] the full moonlight under the walls and on the lanes of the City;[5] or the glory of early dawn on the shores of Galilee.[6] He who has walked and not merely ridden over the land, who has felt its ups and downs, and seen it from the same lowly angle as they who followed the Master on foot, will know how truthfully the painter has dealt with the roads, the fields, the wells, the ribs and scalps of rock, the further

---

[1] No. 14.   [2] No. 42.   [3] No. 22.   [4] No. 54.   [5] No. 76.   [6] No. 78.

slopes and summits, all the immemorial foregrounds and horizons.

The atmosphere and the land have not materially changed. There may have been a slight, yet only a slight, diminution in the rainfall such as is known to have taken place in other regions of the great Mediterranean basin. But to judge from the records of the Bible and the Mishna, the climate, with this possible small exception, is the same to-day as it was in the times of the Prophets and of our Lord. The land was more cultivated then than now. On the hill-slopes the soil was more carefully husbanded by means of terraces easily constructed upon the usually level strata of the lime-stone. Gardens, vineyards and oliveyards were more frequent round Jerusalem and elsewhere; and have been, therefore, warrantably introduced into the pictures in greater numbers[1] than the traveller of to-day will find them. The cultivation, which has been restored chiefly by modern Christians, to several landscapes such as Ain Kârim, the neighbourhood of Bethlehem, and the slopes of Carmel, suggests a more just idea of the ancient conditions of the land as a whole than do the stripped and stony slopes which disappoint the student of the Bible in so many a famous neighbourhood. Yet even upon such slopes (as for instance round Tekoa) the ruined terraces and the abandoned cisterns and wine-presses testify to the almost universal care with which the land was once cultivated. The country is, I repeat, pretty much what it was in Biblical times, save for a greater leanness; more of its ribs and other bones showing through its skin in all the hilly regions. But to balance this a deeper alluvium lies in the valleys and basins. Most of what the hills have lost is gathered here; in Palestine

---

[1] For example, No 31.

there is no river to have swept an appreciable amount of the soil out to sea. Nor do I believe that the wild woodland was ever much greater than we now see it. Outside the Lebanons, Bashan and Carmel there were no forests properly so called. The word translated "forest" in the Old Testament means rather "bush": the loose jungle into which fields tend to lapse with the failure of cultivation. But "the pride" or "rankness" (wrongly translated by our versions "the swelling") of Jordan, the thick growth of trees and underwood which fills the wider bed of the river, was always there; exactly as Mr. Hole has pictured it.[1] Elsewhere it is the large single tree or group of large trees, preserved because of their sanctity as the dwelling-place or whispering oracle of the local deities, which alone are reflected in the Bible, and which still refresh the traveller's eye. Of these, the sycomore which Zacchæus has climbed, and the palm by Capernaum on the Lake of Gennesaret are true types, native to the respective positions on which the artist has planted them.[2]

The romance, the mystery and the gloom of nature, which the poetry of Northern Europe has drawn from the vast forests of that part of the world, had to be sought by the poets of Palestine in other and very different scenes. Above ground were the Sea and the Desert with their storms. The Sea, to which are due so many of the dire and awful imaginations of psalmists and prophets, is absent from the scenery of our Lord's life. The Desert ran close to the life of Judæa: awful, not only in its desolation, but in its pathlessness and in the demonic temptations with which it was believed to be thronged. The school of many of the Hebrew prophets, it supplied them with their most dread pictures of judgment and of death. As

---

[1] No. 17.   [2] Nos. 29, 50, 35.

the scene of our Lord's Temptation its horrors have been vividly suggested by Mr. Hole, in his picture of the ravine in which traditions have placed that crisis.[1]   But the desolation of the Desert is not confined to itself.   No gloom is more oppressive than that which is carried by its hot breath, the sirocco, and by the clouds of sand that accompany this, across the fields and towns of Judæa; as Mr. Hole lets us feel in his picture of Calvary.[2]   But the Hebrew poets felt an even more awful region of mystery beneath their feet in "the Great Deep," whose tides, according to the popular cosmogony of the time, swept underneath the fabric of the earth.   Like the Sea, however, this does not appear in the Gospel history, and if it did what painting could suggest it ?

For the rest, the atmosphere of Palestine is one in which there is but little glamour or mirage.   There is the spell which the sunset throws upon the Moab range as seen from Jerusalem, lessening its apparent distance, and lifting it purple and dominant above the wilderness of Judah, till one forgets that the deep gulf of the Dead Sea lies between.   There is the spell of the orange moon rising from behind the same range and revealing again that weird and awful gulf.   There is the unearthly beauty of the morning mists among the hills of Ephraim, and the glory of the dawn, as Mr. Hole enables us to see it, on the shores of the Lake of Galilee.[3]   But these touches of natural magic are fleeting, and the prevailing impression is of a bare landscape beneath an atmosphere in which there is no illusion.   Light not mystery, charm not grandeur, a homely and not an ethereal beauty, are characteristic of most of the scenery.   Where human life enters, its features are nearly always flat and poor, and not seldom

---

[1] No. 15.   [2] No. 70.   [3] No. 78.

squalid. There is nothing in the light to transform the details of life and death which lie raw and naked beneath it. All these governing tones of the scenery of Palestine appear in the landscapes of the prophets and psalmists; and the pictures of Mr. Hole, in my opinion, faithfully reproduce them. The land and its air seldom suggest the supernatural.

For the ancient architecture of Palestine the modern artist is not without extant models and instructions; but these are of unequal value. The architecture which domi-nated the Jerusalem of our Lord's time was the Herodian. In all the history of Israel no king built so lavishly as Herod did. Nearly all the public buildings of the City, when Jesus taught there, were fresh from the hands of Herod's architects; and whatever amount of ancient material the city walls included, they also without doubt bore the stamp of his vigilance and his enterprise. The Jews them-selves were not a nation of builders, and though some of the lower courses of the walls in Jerusalem, reasonably attributed to Herod, bear Phoenician letters upon them, and therefore were erected by Semitic workmen, it is certain that Herod's architecture as a whole was due to Greek master-builders, or at least was composed under Greek influence and according to Greek models. This is proved both by its surviving remains and by the accounts of it which Josephus has given us. In the solid base of what is now called David's Tower, but which is certainly the platform of Herod's Tower Phasael, Greek influence, says Sir Charles Wilson, "is very apparent . . . . The beautifully dressed and jointed stones of the sloping revetment are essentially Greek in character." But Herod's Hellenic sympathies were still more apparent in his civil and religious buildings. There had been a gym-nasium in Jerusalem as early as the time of the Maccabees; a covered colonnade, called Xystus from its polished floor on which athletes exercised in wintry weather, is several times noticed by Josephus to the west of the Temple beneath the palace of the Hasmonæans on the western hill. Josephus tells us that Herod built a theatre in Jerusalem and an amphi-theatre in the plain. The same writer's description of Herod's Palace implies that at least in part this was Hellenic in style; and it was in Herod's Palace, most probably, that the Roman procurators fixed their Prætorium, and from the front of it that Pontius Pilate uttered his judgment upon Christ. The colonnades of the Temple were also after Greek models, that on the south side having 162 pillars, with Corinthian capitals. They have all vanished. But the surviving monuments in the Valley of the Kidron, with the tomb of Queen Helena of Adiabene, now called the Tombs of the Kings, and certain details in the walls uncovered by Dr. Bliss on the south-west hill of the city's site, furnish the artist with examples of the lines and ornaments followed by the builders of the time. Artists are right, therefore, who represent the public archi-tecture of Jerusalem in New Testament times as dominated by a Greek style. Doubtless also there was much more verdure visible among the buildings than there is now: gardens, groves, arbours and single trees. With regard to the domestic archi-tecture the artist has not the same amount of literary or archæo-logical evidence as he has for the public buildings; and for the most part is left to select for his pictures of private houses and common streets the most ancient-looking building he can find to-day; under the caution to omit from his selection everything that is obviously Byzantine or Saracenic. In Josephus we have evidence that there were many large and handsome private residences in the "Tyrian" style. The dwellings of persons of more moderate means and the houses

the scarlet or purple cloak which the soldiers put on Christ
in mockery of His Kingship are the only two instances of these
colours in wearing-apparel. Blue and green, so common
to-day, the latter as a colour sacred to Islam, are nowhere
mentioned. Women's clothes are a subject of much greater
uncertainty. Probably in this also there has been little change
among the humbler classes. But I have often wondered
whether the distinctive dress of the Christian women of
Bethlehem is not, in part at least, due to Frank fashions in the
time of the Crusades.

The life behind the dress is the same now as then in
attitude, gesture and movement. Thus, for instance, the
pilgrim of to-day must have seen in many Khans the very
inn-keeper whose burly form fills the doorway of the inn at
Bethlehem in which *there was no room ;*[1] and at every difficulty
which he encountered in a strange place just such a boy would
push forward as the one who tells Joseph of the empty stall
and manger. I have seen exactly such a father leading wife
and child upon an ass to ford a stream across their road, as is
shown in the return of the Holy Family from Egypt.[2] The
lithe, upright figures of women with the heavy water-jars upon
their heads are no less happily rendered[3] than the gestures of
the shop-keepers sitting by their stalls, and the customers
crowding round.[4] The procession on which Zacchæus looks
down from his tree,[5] and the crowds which Bartimæus hears
coming along the road,[6] or which accompany our Lord on His
entry into Jerusalem,[7] have the same front and swing as
processions and crowds show to-day upon the roads of the
Land and have always shown. So that it is not only truthfulness of an archæological kind which the pictures evince, but

---

[1] No. 3. [2] No. 9. [3] No. 10. [4] No 36. [5] No. 50. [6] No. 51. [7] No. 52.

the deeper and more urgent authenticity of the common unchanged life of the people among whom our Lord lived and laboured. And this authenticity, which pervades all the pictures, gives them their freshness and is bound to assist in breaking up those flat, stale views of our Lord's life, which we form so conventionally, and to give us a real vision of its circumstance and happening.

But, I repeat, this truth of detail, this near sight of actual things, is not allowed to conflict with the wise and reverent reserve which governs the treatment of the more solemn and difficult scenes and is so impressive in the most sacred of them all: Gethsemane.[1] Here Mr. Hole has worked from the same distance as made his painting, many years ago, of the same subject, so sufficient and memorable. Our great High Priest entered that Holy of Holies alone, leaving behind him even his three most intimate disciples, and the artist has rightly not dared to take us even so near as they went.

GEORGE ADAM SMITH.

---

[1] No 57.

"JESUS OF NAZARETH"

THE BIBLICAL NARRATIVE

No. 1.

NOW in the sixth month the angel Gabriel was sent from God unto a city of Galilee, named Nazareth, to a virgin betrothed to a man whose name was Joseph, of the house of David; and the virgin's name was Mary. And he came in unto her, and said, Hail, thou that art highly favoured, the Lord *is* with thee. But she was greatly troubled at the saying, and cast in her mind what manner of salutation this might be. And the angel said unto her, Fear not, Mary: for thou hast found favour with God. And behold, thou shalt conceive in thy womb, and bring forth a son, and shalt call his name JESUS. He shall be great, and shall be called the Son of the Most High: and the Lord God shall give unto him the throne of his father David: and he shall reign over the house of Jacob for ever; and of his kingdom there shall be no end. And Mary said unto the angel, How shall this be, seeing I know not a man? And the angel answered and said unto her, The Holy Ghost shall come upon thee, and the power of the Most High shall overshadow thee: wherefore also that which is to be born shall be called holy, the Son of God. And behold, Elisabeth thy kinswoman, she also hath conceived a son in her old age: and this is the sixth month with her that was called barren. For no word from God shall be void of power. And Mary said, Behold, the handmaid of the Lord; be it unto me according to thy word. And the angel departed from her.—*S. Luke I. 26-38.*

No. 2.

AND Mary arose in these days and went into the hill country with haste, into a city of Judah; and entered into the house of Zacharias and saluted Elisabeth. And it came to pass, when Elisabeth heard the salutation of Mary, the babe leaped in her womb; and Elisabeth was filled with the Holy Ghost; and she lifted up her voice with a loud cry, and said, Blessed *art* thou among women, and blessed *is* the fruit of thy womb. And whence is this to me, that the mother of my Lord should come unto me? For behold, when the voice of thy salutation came into mine ears, the babe leaped in my womb for joy. And blessed *is* she that believed; for there shall be a fulfilment of the things which have been spoken to her from the Lord. And Mary said,

My soul doth magnify the Lord,
And my spirit hath rejoiced in God my Saviour.
For he hath looked upon the low estate of his handmaiden:
For behold, from henceforth all generations shall call me blessed.
For he that is mighty hath done to me great things;
And holy is his name.
And his mercy is unto generations and generations
On them that fear him.
He hath shewed strength with his arm;
He hath scattered the proud in the imagination of their heart.
He hath put down princes from *their* thrones,
And hath exalted them of low degree.
The hungry he hath filled with good things;
And the rich he hath sent empty away.
He hath holpen Israel his servant,
That he might remember mercy
(As he spake unto our fathers)
Toward Abraham and his seed for ever.

And Mary abode with her about three months, and returned unto her house.—*S. Luke I. 39-56.*

No. 3.

AND Joseph went up from Galilee, out of the city of Nazareth, into Judæa, to the city of David, which is called Bethlehem, because he was of the house and family of David; to enrol himself with Mary, who was betrothed to him, being great with child. And it came to pass, while they were there, the days were fulfilled that she should be delivered. And she brought forth her first-born son; and she wrapped him in swaddling clothes, and laid him in a manger, because there was no room for them in the inn.

S. Luke II. 4–7.

No. 4.

AND there were shepherds in the same country abiding in the field, and keeping watch by night over their flock. And an angel of the Lord stood by them, and the glory of the Lord shone round about them: and they were sore afraid. And the angel said unto them, Be not afraid; for behold, I bring you good tidings of great joy which shall be to all the people: for there is born to you this day in the city of David a Saviour, which is Christ the Lord. And this *is* the sign unto you; Ye shall find a babe wrapped in swaddling clothes, and lying in a manger. And suddenly there was with the angel a multitude of the heavenly host praising God, and saying,

Glory to God in the highest,

And on earth peace among men in whom he is well pleased.

S. Luke II. 8–14.

No. 5.

AND it came to pass, when the angels went away from them into heaven, the shepherds said one to another, Let us now go even unto Bethlehem, and see this thing that is come to pass, which the Lord hath made known unto us. And they came with haste, and found both Mary and Joseph, and the babe lying in the manger.

S. Luke II. 15, 16.

No. 6.

AND when the days of their purification according to the law of Moses were fulfilled, they brought him up to Jerusalem, to present him to the Lord (as it is written in the law of the Lord, Every male that openeth the womb shall be called holy to the Lord), and to offer a sacrifice according to that which is said in the law of the Lord, A pair of turtledoves, or two young pigeons. And behold, there was a man in Jerusalem, whose name was Simeon; and this man was righteous and devout, looking for the consolation of Israel: and the Holy Spirit was upon him. And it had been revealed unto him by the Holy Spirit, that he should not see death, before he had seen the Lord's Christ. And he came in the Spirit into the temple: and when the parents brought in the child Jesus, that they might do concerning him after the custom of the law, then he received him into his arms, and blessed God, and said,

Now lettest thou thy servant depart, O Lord,
According to thy word, in peace;
For mine eyes have seen thy salvation,
Which thou hast prepared before the face of all peoples;
A light for revelation to the Gentiles,
And the glory of thy people Israel.

S. Luke II. 22–32.

No. 7.

NOW when Jesus was born in Bethlehem of Judæa in the days of Herod the king, behold, wise men from the east came to Jerusalem, saying, Where is he that is born King of the Jews? for we saw his star in the east, and are come to worship him.—*S. Matt. II. 1, 2.*

No. 8.

AND lo, the star, which they saw in the east, went before
them, till it came and stood over where the young
child was. And when they saw the star, they rejoiced with
exceeding great joy. And they came into the house and saw
the young child with Mary his mother; and they fell down
and worshipped him; and opening their treasures they
offered unto him gifts, gold and frankincense and myrrh.

S. Matt. II. 9–11.

No. 9.

NOW when they were departed, behold, an angel of the Lord appeareth to Joseph in a dream, saying, Arise and take the young child and his mother, and flee into Egypt, and be thou there until I tell thee: for Herod will seek the young child to destroy him. And he arose and took the young child and his mother by night, and departed into Egypt; and was there until the death of Herod: that it might be fulfilled which was spoken by the Lord through the prophet, saying, Out of Egypt did I call my son. . . . But when Herod was dead, behold, an angel of the Lord appeareth in a dream to Joseph in Egypt, saying, Arise and take the young child and his mother, and go into the land of Israel: for they are dead that sought the young child's life. And he arose and took the young child and his mother, and came into the land of Israel. But when he heard that Archelaus was reigning over Judæa in the room of his father Herod, he was afraid to go thither; and being warned *of God* in a dream, he withdrew into the parts of Galilee, and came and dwelt in a city called Nazareth: that it might be fulfilled which was spoken by the prophets, that he should be called a Nazarene.—*S. Matt. II. 13-15; 19-23.*

No. 10.

AND the child grew, and waxed strong, filled with wisdom: and the grace of God was upon him.—*S. Luke II. 40.*

No. 11.

AND his parents went every year to Jerusalem at the feast of the passover. And when he was twelve years old, they went up after the custom of the feast; and when they had fulfilled the days, as they were returning, the boy Jesus tarried behind in Jerusalem; and his parents knew it not; but supposing him to be in the company, they went a day's journey; and they sought for him among their kinsfolk and acquaintance: and when they found him not, they returned to Jerusalem, seeking for him. And it came to pass, after three days they found him in the temple, sitting in the midst of the doctors, both hearing them, and asking them questions: and all that heard him were amazed at his understanding and his answers. And when they saw him, they were astonished: and his mother said unto him, Son, why hast thou thus dealt with us? behold, thy father and I sought thee sorrowing. And he said unto them, How is it that ye sought me? wist ye not that I must be in my Father's house? And they understood not the saying which he spake unto them.

S. Luke II. 41–50.

No. 12.

AND he went down with them, and came to Nazareth: and he was subject unto them: and his mother kept all *these* sayings in her heart.

And Jesus advanced in wisdom and stature, and in favour with God and men.—*S. Luke II. 51, 52.*

No. 13.

THEN cometh Jesus from Galilee to the Jordan unto John, to be baptized of him. . . . And John bare witness, saying, I have beheld the Spirit descending as a dove out of heaven; and it abode upon him. And I knew him not: but he that sent me to baptize with water, he said unto me, Upon whomsoever thou shalt see the Spirit descending, and abiding upon him, the same is he that baptizeth with the Holy Spirit. And I have seen, and have borne witness that this is the Son of God.—*S. Matt. III. 13 ; S. John I. 32–34.*

No. 14.

THEN was Jesus led up of the Spirit into the wilderness to be tempted of the devil.—*S. Matt. IV. 1.*

No. 15.

AND he was in the wilderness forty days tempted of Satan.—*S. Mark I. 13*

No. 17.

JOHN was standing, and two of his disciples; and he looked upon Jesus as he walked, and saith, Behold, the Lamb of God! And the two disciples heard him speak, and they followed Jesus. And Jesus turned, and beheld them following, and saith unto them, What seek ye? And they said unto him, Rabbi (which is to say, being interpreted, Master), where abidest thou? He saith unto them, Come, and ye shall see. They came therefore and saw where he abode; and they abode with him that day: it was about the tenth hour. One of the two that heard John *speak*, and followed him, was Andrew, Simon Peter's brother. He findeth first his own brother Simon, and saith unto him, We have found the Messiah (which is, being interpreted, Christ). He brought him unto Jesus. Jesus looked upon him, and said, Thou art Simon the son of John: thou shalt be called Cephas (which is by interpretation, Peter).—*S. John I. 35-42.*

No. 18

ON the morrow he was minded to go forth into Galilee, and he findeth Philip: and Jesus saith unto him, Follow me. Now Philip was from Bethsaida, of the city of Andrew and Peter. Philip findeth Nathanael, and saith unto him, We have found him, of whom Moses in the law, and the prophets, did write, Jesus of Nazareth, the son of Joseph.

S. John I. 43–45.

No. 19.

AND the third day there was a marriage in Cana of Galilee; and the mother of Jesus was there: and Jesus also was bidden, and his disciples, to the marriage. And when the wine failed, the mother of Jesus saith unto him, They have no wine. And Jesus saith unto her, Woman, what have I to do with thee? mine hour is not yet come. His mother saith unto the servants, Whatsoever he saith unto you, do it. Now there were six waterpots of stone set there after the Jews' manner of purifying, containing two or three firkins apiece, Jesus saith unto them, Fill the waterpots with water. And they filled them up to the brim. And he saith unto them, Draw out now, and bear unto the ruler of the feast. And they bare it. And when the ruler of the feast tasted the water now become wine, and knew not whence it was (but the servants which had drawn the water knew), the ruler of the feast calleth the bridegroom, and saith unto him, Every man setteth on first the good wine; and when *men* have drunk freely, *then* that which is worse: thou hast kept the good wine until now. This beginning of his signs did Jesus in Cana of Galilee, and manifested his glory; and his disciples believed on him.—*S. John II. 1–11.*

No. 20.

AND the passover of the Jews was at hand, and Jesus went up to Jerusalem. And he found in the temple those that sold oxen and sheep and doves, and the changers of money sitting: and he made a scourge of cords, and cast all out of the temple, both the sheep and the oxen; and he poured out the changers' money, and overthrew their tables; and to them that sold the doves he said, Take these things hence; make not my Father's house a house of merchandise.

S. John II. 13–17.

No. 21.

NOW there was a man of the Pharisees, named Nicodemus, a ruler of the Jews: the same came unto him by night, and said to him, Rabbi, we know that thou art a teacher come from God: for no man can do these signs that thou doest, except God be with him. Jesus answered and said unto him, Verily, verily, I say unto thee, Except a man be born anew, he cannot see the kingdom of God. Nicodemus saith unto him, How can a man be born when he is old? can he enter a second time into his mother's womb, and be born? Jesus answered, Verily, verily, I say unto thee, Except a man be born of water and the Spirit, he cannot enter into the kingdom of God.—*S. John III. 1-5.*

No. 22.

AFTER these things Jesus left Judæa, and departed again
into Galilee. And he must needs pass through Samaria.
So he cometh to a city of Samaria, called Sychar, near to the
parcel of ground that Jacob gave to his son Joseph: and
Jacob's well was there. Jesus therefore, being wearied with
his journey, sat thus by the well. It was about the sixth
hour. There cometh a woman of Samaria to draw water:
Jesus saith unto her, Give me to drink. For his disciples
were gone away into the city to buy food. The Samaritan
woman therefore saith unto him, How is it that thou, being
a Jew, askest drink of me, which am a Samaritan woman?
(For Jews have no dealings with Samaritans.) Jesus answered
and said unto her, If thou knewest the gift of God, and who
it is that saith to thee, Give me to drink; thou wouldest have
asked of him, and he would have given thee living water.

S. John IV. 3–10.

No. 23.

AND he came to Nazareth, where he had been brought up: and he entered, as his custom was, into the synagogue on the sabbath day, and stood up to read. And there was delivered unto him the book of the prophet Isaiah. And he opened the book, and found the place where it was written,

The Spirit of the Lord is upon me,

Because he anointed me to preach good tidings to the poor:

He hath sent me to proclaim release to the captives,

And recovering of sight to the blind,

To set at liberty them that are bruised,

To proclaim the acceptable year of the Lord.

And he closed the book, and gave it back to the attendant, and sat down: and the eyes of all in the synagogue were fastened on him. And he began to say unto them, To-day hath this scripture been fulfilled in your ears. And all bare him witness, and wondered at the words of grace which proceeded out of his mouth: and they said, Is not this Joseph's son? And he said unto them, Doubtless ye will say unto me this parable, Physician, heal thyself: whatsoever we have heard done at Capernaum, do also here in thine own country. And he said, Verily I say unto you, No prophet is acceptable in his own country. But of a truth I say unto you, There were many widows in Israel in the days of Elijah, when the heaven was shut up three years and six months, when there came a great famine over all the land; and unto none of them was Elijah sent, but only to Zarephath, in the land of Sidon, unto a woman that was a widow. And there were many lepers in Israel in the time of Elisha the prophet; and none of them was cleansed, but only Naaman the Syrian. And they were all filled with wrath in the synagogue, as they heard these things; and they rose up, and cast him forth out of the city, and led him unto the brow of the hill whereon their city was built, that they might throw him down headlong. But he passing through the midst of them went his way.—*S. Luke IV. 16–30.*

No. 24.

AND they go into Capernaum; and straightway on the sabbath day he entered into the synagogue and taught. And they were astonished at his teaching: for he taught them as having authority, and not as the scribes. . . . . And at even, when the sun did set, they brought unto him all that were sick, and them that were possessed with devils. And all the city was gathered together at the door. And he healed many that were sick with divers diseases, and cast out many devils; and he suffered not the devils to speak, because they knew him.—*S. Mark I. 21, 22; 32-34.*

No. 25.

AND again he began to teach by the sea side. And there is gathered unto him a very great multitude, so that he entered into a boat, and sat in the sea; and all the multitude were by the sea on the land. And he taught them many things in parables, and said unto them in his teaching, Hearken: Behold, the sower went forth to sow: and it came to pass, as he sowed, some *seed* fell by the way side, and the birds came and devoured it. And other fell on the rocky *ground*, where it had not much earth; and straightway it sprang up, because it had no deepness of earth: and when the sun was risen, it was scorched; and because it had no root, it withered away. And other fell among the thorns, and the thorns grew up, and choked it, and it yielded no fruit. And others fell into the good ground, and yielded fruit, growing up and increasing; and brought forth, thirtyfold, and sixtyfold, and a hundredfold. And he said, Who hath ears to hear, let him hear.—*S. Mark IV. 1-9.*

No. 26.

AND when he had left speaking, he said unto Simon, Put
out into the deep, and let down your nets for a draught.
And Simon answered and said, Master, we toiled all night,
and took nothing: but at thy word I will let down the nets.
And when they had this done, they inclosed a great multitude
of fishes; and their nets were breaking; and they beckoned
unto their partners in the other boat, that they should come
and help them. And they came, and filled both the boats,
so that they began to sink.—*S. Luke V. 4–7.*

No. 27.

AND after these things he went forth, and beheld a publican, named Levi, sitting at the place of toll, and said unto him, Follow me. And he forsook all, and rose up and followed him.—*S. Luke V. 27, 28.*

No. 28.

AND it came to pass in these days, that he went out into the mountain to pray; and he continued all night in prayer to God. And when it was day, he called his disciples: and he chose from them twelve, whom also he named apostles; Simon, whom he also named Peter, and Andrew his brother, and James and John, and Philip and Bartholomew, and Matthew and Thomas, and James *the son* of Alphæus, and Simon which was called the Zealot, and Judas *the son* of James, and Judas Iscariot, which was the traitor; and he came down with them, and stood on a level place, and a great multitude of his disciples, and a great number of the people from all Judæa and Jerusalem, and the sea coast of Tyre and Sidon, which came to hear him, and to be healed of their diseases; and they that were troubled with unclean spirits were healed. And all the multitude sought to touch him: for power came forth from him, and healed *them* all. And he lifted up his eyes on his disciples, and said, Blessed *are* ye poor: for yours is the kingdom of God. Blessed *are* ye that hunger now: for ye shall be filled. Blessed *are* ye that weep now: for ye shall laugh. Blessed are ye, when men shall hate you, and when they shall separate you *from their company*, and reproach you, and cast out your name as evil, for the Son of man's sake. Rejoice in that day, and leap *for joy :* for behold, your reward is great in heaven: for in the same manner did their fathers unto the prophets.—*S. Luke VI. 12–23.*

No. 29.

AND when he was come down from the mountain, great multitudes followed him. And behold, there came to him a leper and worshipped him, saying, Lord, if thou wilt, thou canst make me clean. And he stretched forth his hand, and touched him, saying, I will; be thou made clean. And straightway his leprosy was cleansed. And Jesus saith unto him, See thou tell no man; but go thy way, shew thyself to the priest, and offer the gift that Moses commanded, for a testimony unto them.—*S. Matt. VIII. 1-4.*

No. 30.

AND when he was entered into Capernaum, there came unto him a centurion, beseeching him, and saying, Lord, my servant lieth in the house sick of the palsy, grievously tormented. And he saith unto him, I will come and heal him. And the centurion answered and said, Lord, I am not worthy that thou shouldest come under my roof: but only say the word, and my servant shall be healed. For I also am a man under authority, having under myself soldiers: and I say to this one, Go, and he goeth; and to another, Come, and he cometh; and to my servant, Do this, and he doeth it. And when Jesus heard it, he marvelled, and said to them that followed, Verily I say unto you, I have not found so great faith, no, not in Israel. And I say unto you, that many shall come from the east and the west, and shall sit down with Abraham, and Isaac, and Jacob, in the kingdom of heaven: but the sons of the kingdom shall be cast forth into the outer darkness: there shall be the weeping and gnashing of teeth. And Jesus said unto the centurion, Go thy way; as thou hast believed, so be it done unto thee. And the servant was healed in that hour.

S. Matt. VIII. 5–13.

No. 31.

AND it came to pass soon afterwards, that he went to a
city called Nain; and his disciples went with him, and
a great multitude. Now when he drew near to the gate of
the city, behold, there was carried out one that was dead,
the only son of his mother, and she was a widow: and much
people of the city was with her. And when the Lord saw
her, he had compassion on her, and said unto her, Weep
not. And he came nigh and touched the bier: and the bearers
stood still. And he said, Young man, I say unto thee, Arise.
And he that was dead sat up, and began to speak. And he
gave him to his mother. And fear took hold on all: and
they glorified God, saying, A great prophet is arisen among
us: and, God hath visited his people.—*S. Luke VII. 11–16.*

No. 32.

AND one of the Pharisees desired him that he would eat with him. And he entered into the Pharisee's house, and sat down to meat. And behold, a woman which was in the city, a sinner; and when she knew that he was sitting at meat in the Pharisee's house, she brought an alabaster cruse of ointment, and standing behind at his feet, weeping, she began to wet his feet with her tears, and wiped them with the hair of her head, and kissed his feet, and anointed them with the ointment. Now when the Pharisee which had bidden him saw it, he spake within himself, saying, This man, if he were a prophet, would have perceived who and what manner of woman this is which toucheth him, that she is a sinner. And Jesus answering said unto him, Simon, I have somewhat to say unto thee. And he saith, Master, say on. A certain lender had two debtors: the one owed five hundred pence, and the other fifty. When they had not *wherewith* to pay, he forgave them both. Which of them therefore will love him most? Simon answered and said, He, I suppose, to whom he forgave the most. And he said unto him, Thou hast rightly judged. And turning to the woman, he said unto Simon, Seest thou this woman? I entered into thine house, thou gavest me no water for my feet: but she hath wetted my feet with her tears, and wiped them with her hair. Thou gavest me no kiss: but she, since the time I came in, hath not ceased to kiss my feet. My head with oil thou didst not anoint: but she hath anointed my feet with ointment. Wherefore I say unto thee, Her sins, which are many, are forgiven; for she loved much: but to whom little is forgiven, *the same* loveth little. And he said unto her, Thy sins are forgiven. And they that sat at meat with him began to say within themselves, Who is this that even forgiveth sins? And he said unto the woman, Thy faith hath saved thee; go in peace.—*S. Luke VII. 36–50.*

No. 33.

NOW it came to pass on one of those days, that he entered into a boat, himself and his disciples; and he said unto them, Let us go over unto the other side of the lake: and they launched forth. But as they sailed he fell asleep: and there came down a storm of wind on the lake; and they were filling *with water,* and were in jeopardy. And they came to him, and awoke him, saying, Master, master, we perish. And he awoke, and rebuked the wind and the raging of the water: and they ceased, and there was a calm. And he said unto them, Where is your faith? And being afraid they marvelled, saying one to another, Who then is this, that he commandeth even the winds and the water, and they obey him?—*S. Luke VIII. 22-25.*

No. 34.

AND they arrived at the country of the Gerasenes, which is over against Galilee. And when he was come forth upon the land, there met him a certain man out of the city, who had devils; and for a long time he had worn no clothes, and abode not in *any* house, but in the tombs. And when he saw Jesus, he cried out, and fell down before him, and with a loud voice said, What have I to do with thee, Jesus, thou Son of the Most High God? I beseech thee, torment me not. For he commanded the unclean spirit to come out from the man. For oftentimes it had seized him: and he was kept under guard, and bound with chains and fetters; and breaking the bands asunder, he was driven of the devil into the deserts. And Jesus asked him, What is thy name? And he said, Legion; for many devils were entered into him. And they intreated him that he would not command them to depart into the abyss. Now there was there a herd of many swine feeding on the mountain: and they intreated him that he would give them leave to enter into them. And he gave them leave. And the devils came out from the man, and entered into the swine: and the herd rushed down the steep into the lake, and were choked. And when they that fed them saw what had come to pass, they fled, and told it in the city and in the country. And they went out to see what had come to pass; and they came to Jesus, and found the man, from whom the devils were gone out, sitting, clothed and in his right mind, at the feet of Jesus: and they were afraid.—*S. Luke VIII. 26–35.*

No. 35.

AND when he entered again into Capernaum after some days, it was noised that he was in the house. And many were gathered together, so that there was no longer room *for them*, no, not even about the door: and he spake the word unto them. And they come, bringing unto him a man sick of the palsy, borne of four. And when they could not come nigh unto him for the crowd, they uncovered the roof where he was: and when they had broken it up, they let down the bed whereon the sick of the palsy lay. And Jesus seeing their faith saith unto the sick of the palsy, Son, thy sins are forgiven. But there were certain of the scribes sitting there, and reasoning in their hearts, Why doth this man thus speak? he blasphemeth: who can forgive sins but one, *even* God? And straightway Jesus, perceiving in his spirit that they so reasoned within themselves, saith unto them, Why reason ye these things in your hearts? Whether is easier, to say to the sick of the palsy, Thy sins are forgiven; or to say, Arise, and take up thy bed, and walk? But that ye may know that the Son of man hath power on earth to forgive sins (he saith to the sick of the palsy), I say unto thee, Arise, take up thy bed, and go unto thy house. And he arose, and straightway took up the bed, and went forth before them all; insomuch that they were all amazed, and glorified God, saying, We never saw it on this fashion.—*S. Mark II. 1-12.*

No. 36.

AND there cometh one of the rulers of the synagogue, Jaïrus by name; and seeing him, he falleth at his feet, and beseecheth him much, saying, My little daughter is at the point of death: *I pray thee*, that thou come and lay thy hands on her, that she may be made whole, and live. And he went with him; and a great multitude followed him, and they thronged him. And a woman, which had an issue of blood twelve years, and had suffered many things of many physicians, and had spent all that she had, and was nothing bettered, but rather grew worse, having heard the things concerning Jesus, came in the crowd behind, and touched his garment. For she said, If I touch but his garments, I shall be made whole. And straightway the fountain of her blood was dried up; and she felt in her body that she was healed of her plague. And straightway Jesus, perceiving in himself that the power *proceeding* from him had gone forth, turned him about in the crowd, and said, Who touched my garments? And his disciples said unto him, Thou seest the multitude thronging thee, and sayest thou, Who touched me? And he looked round about to see her that had done this thing. But the woman fearing and trembling, knowing what had been done to her, came and fell down before him, and told him all the truth. And he said unto her, Daughter, thy faith hath made thee whole; go in peace, and be whole of thy plague.—*S. Mark V. 22-34.*

No. 37.

WHILE he yet spake, they come from the ruler of the synagogue's *house*, saying, Thy daughter is dead: why troublest thou the Master any further? But Jesus, not heeding the word spoken, saith unto the ruler of the synagogue, Fear not, only believe. And he suffered no man to follow with him, save Peter, and James, and John the brother of James. And they come to the house of the ruler of the synagogue; and he beholdeth a tumult, and *many* weeping and wailing greatly. And when he was entered in, he saith unto them, Why make ye a tumult, and weep? the child is not dead, but sleepeth. And they laughed him to scorn. But he, having put them all forth, taketh the father of the child and her mother and them that were with him, and goeth in where the child was. And taking the child by the hand, he saith unto her, Talitha cumi; which is, being interpreted, Damsel, I say unto thee, Arise. And straightway the damsel rose up, and walked; for she was twelve years old. And they were amazed straightway with a great amazement. And he charged them much that no man should know this: and he commanded that *something* should be given her to eat.—*S. Mark V.* 35–43.

No. 38.

NOW there is in Jerusalem by the sheep *gate* a pool, which is called in Hebrew Bethesda, having five porches. In these lay a multitude of them that were sick, blind, halt, withered. And a certain man was there, which had been thirty and eight years in his infirmity. When Jesus saw him lying, and knew that he had been now a long time *in that case*, he saith unto him, Wouldest thou be made whole? The sick man answered him, Sir, I have no man, when the water is troubled, to put me into the pool: but while I am coming, another steppeth down before me. Jesus saith unto him, Arise, take up thy bed, and walk. And straightway the man was made whole, and took up his bed and walked.—*S. John* V. *2-9*

No. 39.

AND he saith unto them, Come ye yourselves apart into a desert place, and rest awhile. For there were many coming and going, and they had no leisure so much as to eat. And they went away in the boat to a desert place apart. And *the people* saw them going, and many knew *them,* and they ran there together on foot from all the cities, and outwent them. And he came forth and saw a great multitude, and he had compassion on them, because they were as sheep not having a shepherd: and he began to teach them many things. And when the day was now far spent, his disciples came unto him, and said, The place is desert, and the day is now far spent: send them away, that they may go into the country and villages round about, and buy themselves somewhat to eat. But he answered and said unto them, Give ye them to eat. And they say unto him, Shall we go and buy two hundred pennyworth of bread, and give them to eat? And he saith unto them, How many loaves have ye? go *and* see. And when they knew, they say, Five, and two fishes. And he commanded them that all should sit down by companies upon the green grass. And they sat down in ranks, by hundreds, and by fifties. And he took the five loaves and the two fishes, and looking up to heaven, he blessed, and brake the loaves; and he gave to the disciples to set before them; and the two fishes divided he among them all. And they did all eat, and were filled. And they took up broken pieces, twelve basketfuls, and also of the fishes. And they that ate the loaves were five thousand men.

S. Mark VI. 31–44.

No. 40.

AND straightway he constrained his disciples to enter into the boat, and to go before *him* unto the other side to Bethsaida, while he himself sendeth the multitude away. And after he had taken leave of them, he departed into the mountain to pray. And when even was come, the boat was in the midst of the sea, and he alone on the land. And seeing them distressed in rowing, for the wind was contrary unto them, about the fourth watch of the night he cometh unto them, walking on the sea; and he would have passed by them: but they, when they saw him walking on the sea, supposed that it was an apparition, and cried out: for they all saw him, and were troubled. But he straightway spake with them, and saith unto them, Be of good cheer: it is I; be not afraid. And he went up unto them into the boat; and the wind ceased: and they were sore amazed in themselves; for they understood not concerning the loaves, but their heart was hardened.—*S. Mark VI. 45-52.*

No. 41.

AND Jesus went out thence, and withdrew into the parts of Tyre and Sidon. And behold, a Canaanitish woman came out from those borders, and cried, saying, Have mercy on me, O Lord, thou son of David; my daughter is grievously vexed with a devil. But he answered her not a word. And his disciples came and besought him, saying, Send her away; for she crieth after us. But he answered and said, I was not sent but unto the lost sheep of the house of Israel. But she came and worshipped him, saying, Lord, help me. And he answered and said, It is not meet to take the children's bread and cast it to the dogs. But she said, Yea, Lord: for even the dogs eat of the crumbs which fall from their masters' table. Then Jesus answered and said unto her, O woman, great is thy faith: be it done unto thee even as thou wilt. And her daughter was healed from that hour.

S. Matt. XV. 21–28.

No. 42.

NOW when Jesus came into the parts of Cæsarea Philippi, he asked his disciples, saying, Who do men say that the Son of man is? And they said, Some *say* John the Baptist; some, Elijah: and others, Jeremiah, or one of the prophets. He saith unto them, But who say ye that I am? And Simon Peter answered and said, Thou art the Christ, the Son of the living God. And Jesus answered and said unto him, Blessed art thou, Simon Bar-Jonah: for flesh and blood hath not revealed it unto thee, but my Father which is in heaven. And I also say unto thee, that thou art Peter, and upon this rock I will build my church; and the gates of Hades shall not prevail against it. I will give unto thee the keys of the kingdom of heaven: and whatsoever thou shalt bind on earth shall be bound in heaven: and whatsoever thou shalt loose on earth shall be loosed in heaven. Then charged he the disciples that they should tell no man that he was the Christ.—*S. Matt. XVI. 13-20.*

No. 43.

AND after six days Jesus taketh with him Peter, and James, and John his brother, and bringeth them up into a high mountain apart: and he was transfigured before them: and his face did shine as the sun, and his garments became white as the light. And behold, there appeared unto them Moses and Elijah talking with him. And Peter answered, and said unto Jesus, Lord, it is good for us to be here: if thou wilt, I will make here three tabernacles; one for thee, and one for Moses, and one for Elijah. While he was yet speaking, behold, a bright cloud overshadowed them: and behold, a voice out of the cloud, saying, This is my beloved Son, in whom I am well pleased; hear ye him. And when the disciples heard it, they fell on their face, and were sore afraid. And Jesus came and touched them and said, Arise, and be not afraid. And lifting up their eyes, they saw no one, save Jesus only.—*S. Matt. XVII. 1-8.*

No. 44.

AND it came to pass, on the next day, when they were come down from the mountain, a great multitude met him. And behold, a man from the multitude cried, saying, Master, I beseech thee to look upon my son; for he is mine only child: and behold, a spirit taketh him, and he suddenly crieth out; and it teareth him that he foameth, and it hardly departeth from him, bruising him sorely. And I besought thy disciples to cast it out; and they could not. And Jesus answered and said, O faithless and perverse generation, how long shall I be with you, and bear with you? bring hither thy son. And as he was yet a coming, the devil dashed him down, and tare *him* grievously. But Jesus rebuked the unclean spirit, and healed the boy, **and** gave him back to his father.—*S. Luke IX. 37–42.*

No. 45.

AND the scribes and the Pharisees bring a woman taken in adultery; and having set her in the midst, they say unto him, Master, this woman hath been taken in adultery, in the very act. Now in the law Moses commanded us to stone such: what then sayest thou of her? And this they said, tempting him, that they might have *whereof* to accuse him. But Jesus stooped down, and with his finger wrote on the ground. But when they continued asking him, he lifted up himself, and said unto them, He that is without sin among you, let him first cast a stone at her. And again he stooped down, and with his finger wrote on the ground. And they, when they heard it, went out one by one, beginning from the eldest, *even* unto the last: and Jesus was left alone, and the woman, where she was, in the midst. And Jesus lifted up himself, and said unto her, Woman, where are they? did no man condemn thee? And she said, No man, Lord. And Jesus said, Neither do I condemn thee: go thy way; from henceforth sin no more.—*S. John VIII. 3–11.*

No. 46.

AND it came to pass, as they were on the way to Jerusalem, that he was passing through the midst of Samaria and Galilee. And as he entered into a certain village, there met him ten men that were lepers, which stood afar off: and they lifted up their voices, saying, Jesus, Master, have mercy on us. And when he saw them, he said unto them, Go and shew yourselves unto the priests. And it came to pass, as they went, they were cleansed. And one of them, when he saw that he was healed, turned back, with a loud voice glorifying God; and he fell upon his face at his feet, giving him thanks: and he was a Samaritan. And Jesus answering said, Were not the ten cleansed? but where are the nine? Were there none found that returned to give glory to God, save this stranger? And he said unto him, Arise, and go thy way: thy faith hath made thee whole.

S. Luke XVII. 11-19.

No. 47.

NOW as they went on their way, he entered into a certain
village: and a certain woman named Martha received
him into her house. And she had a sister called Mary,
which also sat at the Lord's feet, and heard his word. But
Martha was cumbered about much serving; and she came
up to him, and said, Lord, dost thou not care that my sister
did leave me to serve alone? bid her therefore that she help
me. But the Lord answered and said unto her, Martha,
Martha, thou art anxious and troubled about many things:
but one thing is needful: for Mary hath chosen the good
part, which shall not be taken away from her.

S. Luke X. 38-42.

No. 48.

AND they brought unto him little children, that he should touch them: and the disciples rebuked them. But when Jesus saw it, he was moved with indignation, and said unto them, Suffer the little children to come unto me; forbid them not: for of such is the kingdom of God. Verily I say unto you, Whosoever shall not receive the kingdom of God as a little child, he shall in no wise enter therein. And he took them in his arms, and blessed them, laying his hands upon them.—*S. Mark X. 13-16.*

No. 49.

NOW a certain man was sick, Lazarus of Bethany, of the village
of Mary and her sister Martha. The sisters therefore sent unto
him, saying, Lord, behold, he whom thou lovest is sick. But when
Jesus heard it, he said, This sickness is not unto death, but for the
glory of God, that the Son of God may be glorified thereby. Now
Jesus loved Martha, and her sister, and Lazarus. When therefore he
heard that he was sick, he abode at that time two days in the place
where he was. . . . Then Jesus said unto them plainly, Lazarus
is dead. And I am glad for your sakes that I was not there, to the
intent ye may believe; nevertheless let us go unto him. . . .
Jesus groaning in himself cometh to the tomb. Now it was a cave,
and a stone lay against it. Jesus saith, Take ye away the stone.
Martha, the sister of him that was dead, saith unto him, Lord, by
this time he stinketh: for he hath been *dead* four days. Jesus saith
unto her, Said I not unto thee, that, if thou believedst, thou shouldest
see the glory of God? So they took away the stone. And Jesus
lifted up his eyes, and said, Father, I thank thee that thou heardest
me. And I knew that thou hearest me always: but because of the
multitude which standeth around I said it, that they may believe that
thou didst send me. And when he had thus spoken, he cried with
a loud voice, Lazarus, come forth. He that was dead came forth,
bound hand and foot with grave-clothes; and his face was bound
about with a napkin. Jesus saith unto them, Loose him, and let
him go.—*S. John XI. 1; 3–6; 14, 15; 38–44.*

No. 50.

AND he entered and was passing through Jericho. And behold, a man called by name Zacchæus; and he was a chief publican, and he was rich. And he sought to see Jesus who he was; and could not for the crowd, because he was little of stature. And he ran on before, and climbed up into a sycomore tree to see him: for he was to pass that way. And when Jesus came to the place, he looked up, and said unto him, Zacchæus, make haste, and come down; for to-day I must abide at thy house. And he made haste, and came down, and received him joyfully. And when they saw it, they all murmured, saying, He is gone in to lodge with a man that is a sinner. And Zacchæus stood, and said unto the Lord, Behold, Lord, the half of my goods I give to the poor; and if I have wrongfully exacted aught of any man, I restore fourfold. And Jesus said unto him, To-day is salvation come to this house, forasmuch as he also is a son of Abraham. For the Son of man came to seek and to save that which was lost.—*S. Luke XIX. 1-10.*

No. 53.

AND he was teaching daily in the temple. But the chief priests and the scribes and the principal men of the people sought to destroy him: and they could not find what they might do; for the people all hung upon him, listening. And it came to pass, on one of the days, as he was teaching the people in the temple, and preaching the gospel, there came upon him the chief priests and the scribes with the elders; and they spake, saying unto him, Tell us: By what authority doest thou these things? or who is he that gave thee this authority? And he answered and said unto them, I also will ask you a question; and tell me: The baptism of John, was it from heaven, or from men? And they reasoned with themselves, saying, If we shall say, From heaven; he will say, Why did ye not believe him? But if we shall say, From men; all the people will stone us: for they be persuaded that John was a prophet. And they answered, that they knew not whence *it was*. And Jesus said unto them, Neither tell I you by what authority I do these things.

S. Luke XIX. 47, 48; XX. 1-8.

No. 54.

AND every day he was teaching in the temple; and every
night he went out, and lodged in the mount that is
called *the mount* of Olives.—*S. Luke XXI. 37.*

No. 55.

NOW before the feast of the passover, Jesus knowing that his hour was come that he should depart out of this world unto the Father, having loved his own which were in the world, he loved them unto the end. And during supper, the devil having already put into the heart of Judas Iscariot, Simon's *son*, to betray him, *Jesus*, knowing that the Father had given all things into his hands, and that he came forth from God, and goeth unto God, riseth from supper, and layeth aside his garments; and he took a towel, and girded himself. Then he poureth water into the bason, and began to wash the disciples' feet, and to wipe them with the towel wherewith he was girded. So he cometh to Simon Peter. He saith unto him, Lord, dost thou wash my feet? Jesus answered and said unto him, What I do thou knowest not now; but thou shalt understand hereafter. Peter saith unto him, Thou shalt never wash my feet. Jesus answered him, If I wash thee not, thou hast no part with me. Simon Peter saith unto him, Lord, not my feet only, but also my hands and my head. Jesus saith to him, He that is bathed needeth not save to wash his feet, but is clean every whit: and ye are clean, but not all.—*S. John XIII. 1–10.*

No. 56.

WHEN Jesus had thus said, he was troubled in the spirit, and testified, and said, Verily, verily, I say unto you, that one of you shall betray me. The disciples looked one on another, doubting of whom he spake. There was at the table reclining in Jesus' bosom one of his disciples, whom Jesus loved. Simon Peter therefore beckoneth to him, and saith unto him, Tell *us* who it is of whom he speaketh. He leaning back, as he was, on Jesus' breast saith unto him, Lord, who is it? Jesus therefore answereth, He it is, for whom I shall dip the sop, and give it him. So when he had dipped the sop, he taketh and giveth it to Judas, *the son* of Simon Iscariot. And after the sop, then entered Satan into him. Jesus therefore saith unto him, That thou doest, do quickly. Now no man at the table knew for what intent he spake this unto him. For some thought, because Judas had the bag, that Jesus said unto him, Buy what things we have need of for the feast; or, that he should give something to the poor. He then having received the sop went out straightway: and it was night. . . . . .

And as they were eating, he took bread, and when he had blessed, he brake it, and gave to them, and said, Take ye: this is my body. And he took a cup, and when he had given thanks, he gave to them: and they all drank of it. And he said unto them, This is my blood of the covenant, which is shed for many. Verily I say unto you, I will no more drink of the fruit of the vine, until that day when I drink it new in the kingdom of God.

And when they had sung a hymn, they went out unto the mount of Olives.—*S. John XIII. 21-30—S. Mark XIV. 22-26.*

No. 57.

THEN cometh Jesus with them unto a place called Gethsemane, and saith unto his disciples, Sit ye here, while I go yonder and pray. And he took with him Peter and the two sons of Zebedee, and began to be sorrowful and sore troubled. Then saith he unto them, My soul is exceeding sorrowful, even unto death: abide ye here, and watch with me. And he went forward a little, and fell on his face, and prayed, saying, O my Father, if it be possible, let this cup pass away from me: nevertheless, not as I will, but as thou wilt. And he cometh unto the disciples, and findeth them sleeping, and saith unto Peter, What, could ye not watch with me one hour? Watch and pray, that ye enter not into temptation: the spirit indeed is willing, but the flesh is weak. Again a second time he went away, and prayed, saying, O my Father, if this cannot pass away, except I drink it, thy will be done. And he came again and found them sleeping, for their eyes were heavy. And he left them again, and went away, and prayed a third time, saying again the same words. Then cometh he to the disciples, and saith unto them, Sleep on now, and take your rest: behold, the hour is at hand, and the Son of man is betrayed unto the hands of sinners. Arise, let us be going: behold, he is at hand that betrayeth me.—*S. Matt. XXVI. 36–46.*

No. 58.

JUDAS then, having received the band *of soldiers*, and officers from the chief priests and the Pharisees, cometh thither with lanterns and torches and weapons. Jesus therefore, knowing all the things that were coming upon him, went forth, and saith unto them, Whom seek ye? They answered him, Jesus of Nazareth. Jesus saith unto them, I am *he*. And Judas also, which betrayed him, was standing with them. When therefore he said unto them, I am *he*, they went backward, and fell to the ground.

Now he that betrayed him gave them a sign, saying, Whomsoever I shall kiss, that is he: take him. And straightway he came to Jesus, and said, Hail, Rabbi; and kissed him. And Jesus said unto him, Friend, *do* that for which thou art come. Then they came and laid hands on Jesus, and took him. And behold, one of them that were with Jesus stretched out his hand, and drew his sword, and smote the servant of the high priest, and struck off his ear. Then saith Jesus unto him, Put up again thy sword into its place: for all they that take the sword shall perish with the sword. Or thinkest thou that I cannot beseech my Father, and he shall even now send me more than twelve legions of angels? How then should the scriptures be fulfilled, that thus it must be? In that hour said Jesus to the multitudes, Are ye come out as against a robber with swords and staves to seize me? I sat daily in the temple teaching, and ye took me not. But all this is come to pass, that the scriptures of the prophets might be fulfilled. Then all the disciples left him, and fled.

S. John XVIII. 3–6—S. Matt. XXVI. 48–56.

No. 59.

AND they that had taken Jesus led him away to *the house
of* Caiaphas the high priest, where the scribes and the
elders were gathered together. But Peter followed him afar
off, unto the court of the high priest, and entered in, and sat
with the officers, to see the end. Now the chief priests and
the whole council sought false witness against Jesus, that
they might put him to death; and they found it not, though
many false witnesses came. But afterward came two, and
said, This man said, I am able to destroy the temple of
God, and to build it in three days. And the high priest
stood up, and said unto him, Answerest thou nothing? what
is it which these witness against thee? But Jesus held his
peace. And the high priest said unto him, I adjure thee by
the living God, that thou tell us whether thou be the Christ,
the Son of God. Jesus saith unto him, Thou hast said:
nevertheless I say unto you, Henceforth ye shall see the Son
of man sitting at the right hand of power, and coming on
the clouds of heaven. Then the high priest rent his garments, saying, He hath spoken blasphemy: what further
need have we of witnesses? behold, now ye have heard the
blasphemy: what think ye? They answered and said, He
is worthy of death.—*S. Matt. XXVI. 57–66.*

No. 60.

NOW Peter was sitting without in the court: and a maid came unto him, saying, Thou also wast with Jesus the Galilæan. But he denied before them all, saying, I know not what thou sayest. And when he was gone out into the porch, another *maid* saw him, and saith unto them that were there, This man also was with Jesus the Nazarene. And again he denied with an oath, I know not the man. And after a little while they that stood by came and said to Peter, Of a truth thou also art *one* of them; for thy speech bewrayeth thee. Then began he to curse and to swear, I know not the man. And straightway the cock crew. . . . .

And the Lord turned, and looked upon Peter. And Peter remembered the word of the Lord, how that he said unto him, Before the cock crow this day, thou shalt deny me thrice. And he went out, and wept bitterly.

S. Matt. XXVI. 69–74—S. Luke XXII. 61, 62.

No. 62.

PILATE therefore entered again into the palace, and called
Jesus, and said unto him, Art thou the King of the Jews?
Jesus answered, Sayest thou this of thyself, or did others tell
it thee concerning me? Pilate answered, Am I a Jew? Thine
own nation and the chief priests delivered thee unto me: what
hast thou done? Jesus answered, My kingdom is not of this
world: if my kingdom were of this world, then would my
servants fight, that I should not be delivered to the Jews:
but now is my kingdom not from hence. Pilate therefore
said unto him, Art thou a king then? Jesus answered, Thou
sayest that I am a king. To this end have I been born, and
to this end am I come into the world, that I should bear
witness unto the truth. Every one that is of the truth heareth
my voice. Pilate saith unto him, What is truth?

S. John XVIII. 33–38.

No. 63.

AND Pilate said unto the chief priests and the multitudes, I find no fault in this man. But they were the more urgent, saying, He stirreth up the people, teaching throughout all Judæa, and beginning from Galilee even unto this place. But when Pilate heard it, he asked whether the man were a Galilæan. And when he knew that he was of Herod's jurisdiction, he sent him unto Herod, who himself also was at Jerusalem in these days. Now when Herod saw Jesus, he was exceeding glad: for he was of a long time desirous to see him. because he had heard concerning him; and he hoped to see some miracle done by him. And he questioned him in many words; but he answered him nothing. And the chief priests and the scribes stood, vehemently accusing him. And Herod with his soldiers set him at nought, and mocked him, and arraying him in gorgeous apparel sent him back to Pilate.—*S. Luke XXIII. 4-11.*

No. 65.

THEN the soldiers of the governor took Jesus into the palace, and gathered unto him the whole band. And they stripped him, and put on him a scarlet robe. And they plaited a crown of thorns and put it upon his head, and a reed in his right hand; and they kneeled down before him, and mocked him, saying, Hail, King of the Jews! And they spat upon him, and took the reed and smote him on the head —*S. Matt. XXVII. 27–30.*

No. 66.

AND Pilate went out again, and saith unto them, Behold, I bring him out to you, that ye may know that I find no crime in him. Jesus therefore came out, wearing the crown of thorns and the purple garment. And *Pilate* saith unto them, Behold, the man! When therefore the chief priests and the officers saw him, they cried out, saying, Crucify *him*, crucify *him*. . . . .

And he said, Why, what evil hath he done? But they cried out exceedingly, saying, Let him be crucified. So when Pilate saw that he prevailed nothing, but rather that a tumult was arising, he took water, and washed his hands before the multitude, saying, I am innocent of the blood of this righteous man: see ye *to it*. And all the people answered and said, His blood *be* on us, and on our children. Then released he unto them Barabbas: but Jesus he delivered to be crucified.

S. John XIX. 4–6—S. Matt. XXVII. 23–26.

No. 67.

AND when they led him away, they laid hold upon one Simon of Cyrene, coming from the country, and laid on him the cross, to bear it after Jesus. And there followed him a great multitude of the people, and of women who bewailed and lamented him. But Jesus turning unto them said, Daughters of Jerusalem, weep not for me, but weep for yourselves, and for your children. For behold, the days are coming, in which they shall say, Blessed are the barren, and the wombs that never bare, and the breasts that never gave suck. Then shall they begin to say to the mountains, Fall on us; and to the hills, Cover us. For if they do these things in the green tree, what shall be done in the dry?—*S. Luke XXIII. 26–31.*

No. 68.

AND there were also two others, malefactors, led with him
to be put to death. And when they came unto the place
which is called The skull, there they crucified him, and the
malefactors, one on the right hand and the other on the left.
And Jesus said, Father, forgive them; for they know not
what they do. And parting his garments among them, they
cast lots. And the people stood beholding.

S. Luke XXIII. 32–35.

No. 69.

BUT there were standing by the cross of Jesus his mother, and his mother's sister, Mary the *wife* of Clopas, and Mary Magdalene. When Jesus therefore saw his mother, and the disciple standing by, whom he loved, he saith unto his mother, Woman, behold, thy son! Then saith he to the disciple, Behold, thy mother! And from that hour the disciple took her unto his own *home.—S. John XIX. 25–27.*

No. 70.

AND it was now about the sixth hour, and a darkness came over the whole land until the ninth hour, the sun's light failing: and the veil of the temple was rent in the midst. And when Jesus had cried with a loud voice, he said, Father, into thy hands I commend my spirit: and having said this, he gave up the ghost. And when the centurion saw what was done, he glorified God, saying, Certainly this was a righteous man. And all the multitudes that came together to this sight, when they beheld the things that were done, returned smiting their breasts.—*S. Luke XXIII. 44–48.*

No. 71.

AND behold, a man named Joseph, who was a councillor, a good man and a righteous (he had not consented to their counsel and deed), *a man* of Arimathæa, a city of the Jews, who was looking for the kingdom of God: this man went to Pilate, and asked for the body of Jesus. And he took it down, and wrapped it in a linen cloth, and laid him in a tomb that was hewn in stone, where never man had yet lain. And it was the day of the Preparation, and the sabbath drew on. And the women, which had come with him out of Galilee, followed after, and beheld the tomb, and how his body was laid. And they returned, and prepared spices and ointments.—*S. Luke XXIII. 50–56.*

No. 72.

AND on the sabbath they rested according to the com-
mandment. But on the first day of the week, at early
dawn, they came unto the tomb, bringing the spices which
they had prepared. And they found the stone rolled away
from the tomb. And they entered in, and found not the body
of the Lord Jesus. And it came to pass, while they were
perplexed thereabout, behold, two men stood by them in
dazzling apparel: and as they were affrighted, and bowed
down their faces to the earth, they said unto them, Why
seek ye the living among the dead? He is not here, but is
risen: remember how he spake unto you when he was yet
in Galilee, saying that the Son of man must be delivered up
into the hands of sinful men, and be crucified, and the third
day rise again. And they remembered his words, and returned
from the tomb, and told all these things to the eleven, and
to all the rest.—*S. Luke XXIII. 56; XXIV. 1-9.*

No. 73.

PETER therefore went forth, and the other disciple, and they went toward the tomb. And they ran both together: and the other disciple outran Peter, and came first to the tomb; and stooping and looking in, he seeth the linen cloths lying; yet entered he not in. Simon Peter therefore also cometh, following him, and entered into the tomb; and he beholdeth the linen cloths lying, and the napkin, that was upon his head, not lying with the linen cloths, but rolled up in a place by itself. Then entered in therefore the other disciple also, which came first to the tomb, and he saw, and believed. For as yet they knew not the scripture, that he must rise again from the dead. So the disciples went away again unto their own home.—*S. John XX. 3-10.*

No. 74.

BUT Mary was standing without at the tomb weeping: so, as she wept, she stooped and looked into the tomb; and she beholdeth two angels in white sitting, one at the head, and one at the feet, where the body of Jesus had lain. And they say unto her, Woman, why weepest thou? She saith unto them, Because they have taken away my Lord, and I know not where they have laid him. When she had thus said, she turned herself back, and beholdeth Jesus standing, and knew not that it was Jesus. Jesus saith unto her, Woman, why weepest thou? whom seekest thou? She, supposing him to be the gardener, saith unto him, Sir, if thou hast borne him hence, tell me where thou hast laid him, and I will take him away. Jesus saith unto her, Mary. She turneth herself, and saith unto him in Hebrew, Rabboni; which is to say, Master. Jesus saith to her, Touch me not; for I am not yet ascended unto the Father: but go unto my brethren, and say to them, I ascend unto my Father and your Father, and my God and your God. Mary Magdalene cometh and telleth the disciples, I have seen the Lord; and *how that* he had said these things unto her.

S. John XX. 11–18.

No. 75.

AND behold, two of them were going that very day to a village
named Emmaus, which was threescore furlongs from Jerusalem.
And they communed with each other of all these things which had
happened. And it came to pass, while they communed and questioned
together, that Jesus himself drew near, and went with them. But their
eyes were holden that they should not know him. And he said unto
them, What communications are these that ye have one with another, as
ye walk? And they stood still, looking sad. And one of them, named
Cleopas, answering said unto him, Dost thou alone sojourn in Jerusalem and not know the things which are come to pass there in these
days? And he said unto them, What things? And they said unto
him, The things concerning Jesus of Nazareth, which was a prophet
mighty in deed and word before God and all the people: and how the
chief priests and our rulers delivered him up to be condemned to death,
and crucified him. But we hoped that it was he which should redeem
Israel. Yea and beside all this, it is now the third day since these
things came to pass. Moreover certain women of our company amazed
us, having been early at the tomb; and when they found not his body,
they came, saying, that they had also seen a vision of angels, which
said that he was alive. And certain of them that were with us went
to the tomb, and found it even so as the women had said: but him
they saw not. And he said unto them, O foolish men, and slow of
heart to believe in all that the prophets have spoken! Behoved it not
the Christ to suffer these things, and to enter into his glory? And
beginning from Moses and from all the prophets, he interpreted to them
in all the scriptures the things concerning himself.—*S. Luke XXIV. 13-27.*

No. 76.

AND they drew nigh unto the village, whither they were going: and he made as though he would go further. And they constrained him, saying, Abide with us: for it is toward evening, and the day is now far spent. And he went in to abide with them. And it came to pass, when he had sat down with them to meat, he took the bread, and blessed it, and brake, and gave to them. And their eyes were opened, and they knew him; and he vanished out of their sight. And they said one to another, Was not our heart burning within us, while he spake to us in the way, while he opened to us the scriptures? And they rose up that very hour, and returned to Jerusalem, and found the eleven gathered together, and them that were with them, saying, The Lord is risen indeed, and hath appeared to Simon.—*S. Luke XXIV. 28-34.*

No. 77.

WHEN it was evening, on that day, the first *day* of the week, and when the doors were shut where the disciples were, for fear of the Jews, Jesus came and stood in the midst, and saith unto them, Peace *be* unto you. And when he had said this, he shewed unto them his hands and his side. The disciples therefore were glad, when they saw the Lord. . . . But Thomas, one of the twelve, called Didymus, was not with them when Jesus came. The other disciples therefore said unto him, We have seen the Lord. But he said unto them, Except I shall see in his hands the print of the nails, and put my finger into the print of the nails, and put my hand into his side, I will not believe. And after eight days again his disciples were within, and Thomas with them. Jesus cometh, the doors being shut, and stood in the midst, and said, Peace *be* unto you. Then saith he to Thomas. Reach hither thy finger, and see my hands; and reach *hither* thy hand, and put it into my side: and be not faithless, but believing. Thomas answered and said unto him, My Lord and my God. Jesus saith unto him, Because thou hast seen me, thou hast believed: blessed *are* they that have not seen, and *yet* have believed.

S. John XX. 19, 20 ; 24–29.

No. 78.

AFTER these things Jesus manifested himself again to the disciples at the sea of Tiberias; and he manifested *himself* on this wise. There were together Simon Peter, and Thomas called Didymus, and Nathanael of Cana in Galilee, and the *sons* of Zebedee, and two other of his disciples. Simon Peter saith unto them, I go a fishing. They say unto him, We also come with thee. They went forth, and entered into the boat; and that night they took nothing. But when day was now breaking, Jesus stood on the beach: howbeit the disciples knew not that it was Jesus. Jesus therefore saith unto them, Children, have ye aught to eat? They answered him, No. And he said unto them, Cast the net on the right side of the boat, and ye shall find. They cast therefore, and now they were not able to draw it for the multitude of fishes. That disciple therefore whom Jesus loved saith unto Peter, It is the Lord. So when Simon Peter heard that it was the Lord, he girt his coat about him (for he was naked), and cast himself into the sea. But the other disciples came in the little boat (for they were not far from the land, but about two hundred cubits off), dragging the net *full* of fishes. So when they got out upon the land, they see a fire of coals there, and fish laid thereon, and bread. Jesus saith unto them, Bring of the fish which ye have now taken. Simon Peter therefore went up, and drew the net to land, full of great fishes, a hundred and fifty and three: and for all there were so many, the net was not rent. Jesus saith unto them, Come *and* break your fast. And none of the disciples durst inquire of him, Who art thou? knowing that it was the Lord. Jesus cometh, and taketh the bread, and giveth them, and the fish likewise. This is now the third time that Jesus was manifested to the disciples, after that he was risen from the dead.—*S. John XXI. 1-14.*

No. 79.

AND he led them out until *they were* over against Bethany:
and he lifted up his hands, and blessed them. And it
came to pass, while he blessed them, he parted from them,
and was carried up into heaven. . . . .

And while they were looking stedfastly into heaven as
he went, behold, two men stood by them in white apparel;
which also said, Ye men of Galilee, why stand ye looking
into heaven? this Jesus, which was received up from you
into heaven, shall so come in like manner as ye beheld him
going into heaven.—*S. Luke XXIV. 50, 51—Acts I. 10, 11.*

No. 80.

WHERE two or three are gathered together in my name, there am I in the midst of them.—*S. Matt. XVIII. 20.*

AND lo, I am with you alway, even unto the end of the world.—*S. Matt. XXVIII. 20.*

NOTES ON PICTURES ILLUSTRATING THE LIFE OF JESUS

BY THE ARTIST

1. S. LUKE i. 26–38.—*The Angel Gabriel haileth the Virgin Mary and announceth to her the mystery of the incarnation.*

The Virgin Mary is here represented in the ordinary attire of a woman of the country, kneeling in prayer upon the mat or carpet, which, laid upon the floor, serves the purpose of a bed.

2. S. LUKE i. 39–56.—*Mary goeth into the hill country of Judæa and saluteth Elisabeth.*

The difference of costume worn by women of Northern, and of Southern Palestine is distinctly marked. The Virgin wears the holiday dress of a Nazarene; Elisabeth that of a woman of Bethlehem and its neighbourhood.

3. S. LUKE ii. 4–7.—*Joseph and Mary arrive at Bethlehem, but find there no room for them in the Inn.*

A Syrian Khan or Inn is wholly devoid of privacy. Shallow and unfurnished recesses, open for the most part, and but slightly raised above the level of the ground, provide the sole accommodation for travellers, whose animals with their attendants are crowded together in the central area.

4. S. LUKE ii. 8–14.—*An angel announceth to the Shepherds of Bethlehem the Birth of Jesus.*

Herding sheep was considered by the Jews to be amongst the humblest of occupations; it was assigned, therefore, to bondmen chiefly, and to younger sons.

5. S. LUKE ii. 15, 16.—*Thereupon the Shepherds proceed to Bethlehem and find the babe lying in a manger.*

In households of the humbler class, the family not infrequently share the single apartment with their cattle, occupying, as in the case of the Khan before mentioned, the raised platform or "læwan", in the edge of which is the feeding trough or "manger" for the cattle. Such in all probability was the arrangement of the cave-dwelling at Bethlehem which, according to tradition, provided a refuge for the Holy Family.

6. S. LUKE ii. 22–32.—*The child Jesus, brought to the Temple to be presented to the Lord, is recognised by Simeon as the Saviour.*

The scene is laid at the foot of the fifteen steps which, in Herod's temple, led from the Second Court (the Court of the Women) through the Nicanor Gate to the Inner, or Court of the Priests, in which stood the altar of sacrifice in front of the Temple proper.

NOTES ON PICTURES

7. S. MATT. ii. 1, 2.—*Having seen his Star in the East, three wise men journey to Jerusalem, and enquire for him who is born King of the Jews.*

The space immediately within the city gate is frequently used as a market-place, and that at Jerusalem during the period of Roman occupation would certainly be the post of a military guard.

8. S. MATT. ii. 9–11.—*They arrive at Bethlehem, and worship the child, presenting him with kingly gifts.*

Mediæval tradition, based in the first instance upon a literal acceptance of Isa. lx. 1–3, is responsible for the otherwise unsupported supposition that the "Wise Men" of the Gospel were Kings. It would seem equally justifiable to believe that these may have been holy and humble men of heart, searching towards the Higher Light through the twilight afforded by the three great Eastern religions which bear the names of Brahma, Zoroaster, and Buddha.

9. S. MATT. ii. 13–15, 19–23.—*Warned by God in a dream, Joseph taketh him with his mother into Egypt, whence they return to Nazareth on the death of Herod.*

In a journey such as this, i.e., the return from Egypt, it would be contrary to Eastern use and wont that the woman should ride while her husband walked. Only in cases of sickness or infirmity would such a departure from ordinary custom be deemed justifiable. In Syria, infants are usually carried by their mothers upon the hip, older children upon the shoulder, as in the picture.

10. S. LUKE ii. 40.—*And there his childhood is spent, the grace of God being with him.*

"Ain Miryam" or Mary's Well, is one of the sites of whose authenticity there can be no reasonable doubt. It is the only public fountain in Nazareth, and thither must the Virgin Mother and her child have proceeded daily to draw water for the household.

11. S. LUKE ii. 41–50.—*Jesus goeth up with his parents to the Passover at the age of twelve years, and tarrieth behind in the Temple, seeking instruction from the doctors of the Law.*

Jesus is here represented, making no display of his own learning, but as a searcher after higher wisdom than he as yet possessed. For this purpose, having doubtless exhausted such means of knowledge as could be provided in his provincial home, he eagerly seized the opportunity afforded by his first visit to Jerusalem to attend the theological lectures delivered in one of the "Scholae" of the Temple, adjoining the Court of the Gentiles. Amongst the doctors of the Law who "were astonished at his understanding and answers" may have been the aged Hillel and his great rival Shammai, the Rabban Simeon, Jonathan ben Uzziel, and others whose names are associated with this period of brilliant rabbinical learning. In default of definite knowledge regarding the architectural style of the interior of the Temple, its leading features, in this as in other pictures, are, to a great extent, adapted from those of "the Dome of the Rock," which occupies the same site.

12. S. LUKE ii. 51, 52.—*He returneth with his parents to Nazareth where he is subject unto them.*

Beyond the facts that he was subject to his parents, that he grew in wisdom as he advanced in age, and that he was beloved by all who knew him, the picture illustrates all that we know of the life of Jesus until he attained the age of thirty years. He worked with Joseph as a carpenter at Nazareth, making the simple articles which comprise the furniture of an Eastern home, and, amongst other things, the primitive wooden ploughs still in use in all parts of Palestine.

13. S. MATT. iii. 13—S. JOHN i. 32-34.—*Jesus is baptized in Jordan by John the Baptist who seeth the Spirit of God descend upon him.*

The traditional site of the Baptism in Jordan, about six miles from Jericho, is here accepted and represented;

14. S. MATT. iv. 1.—*The Spirit then driveth Jesus into the wilderness.*

As is also the arid and stony wilderness leading thence to the hill called Quarantania, the traditional scene of the Temptation. On the way, Jesus would approach, or cross, the brook now known as the Wady Kelt, which winds through this desert from a neighbouring gorge until it reaches the Jordan.

15. S. MARK i. 13.—*Where he remaineth fasting forty days and forty nights being tempted of Satan.*

Imagination fails to picture a scene of more terrible desolation and utter solitude than is presented by the ravine which age-long tradition indicates as the spot which witnessed that forty-days' conflict between Good and Evil, the chief crises of which are alone described in the Gospel narrative. Some frightful convulsion of nature would seem to have rent asunder the cliffs which tower on either hand, whilst the eye seeks in vain amongst the rocks and sand slanting precipitously to the bottom of the gorge, for a trace of the scant vegetation which is to be found elsewhere, even in the most arid and waterless districts of the Judæan wilderness.

NOTES ON PICTURES

16. S. MATT. iv. 8–11.—*The temptation being ended, Satan leaveth Jesus.*

Whether a mental or an optical vision of the kingdoms of the world is referred to in the text, it is clearly stated that the last temptation took place upon an "exceeding high mountain"; and as mountains of exceptional altitude are invariably capped with snow, a snow-peak, touched with earliest sunrise, is therefore selected as the scene of Satan's final and greatest effort of temptation, and of its failure.

17. S. JOHN i. 35–42.—*Jesus then returneth to Jordan where John and Andrew follow him, the latter bringing also his brother Simon.*

Jesus' lodging on the banks of the Jordan, at which place his earliest disciples were attracted by his words and teaching, was probably one of those black goat-hair tents in common use among the wandering inhabitants of the "Ghor," or Lower Jordan valley.

18. S. JOHN i. 43–45.—*With these and two other disciples, Philip and Nathanael, Jesus journeyeth into Galilee.*

The scene depicted is familiar to pilgrims, being that known as the Wady Harâmîyeh, a beautiful valley through which runs the road from Jerusalem to Shechem and Galilee. Jesus and his disciples journeying from the Jordan, would probably join this road at Bethel, which lies a few miles to the south.

19. S. JOHN ii. 1–11.—*Where he is present at a marriage feast in Cana, and performeth his first miracle.*

The typical Syrian house of the better class, which has been selected for this illustration, partly surrounds the central quadrangle, the other two sides of which are guarded by high walls. Two women, grinding at the mill, are seated in the flickering shade of an almond tree, at the entrance of the kitchen, which with other offices occupies the basement of the dwelling; while servants bearing dishes for the feast ascend by an outside stair to the guest-chamber or "large upper room." A carrier replenishes the jars from the goatskin bag or "bottle" in which he has brought water from the public cistern.

20. S. JOHN ii. 13–17.—*Jesus goeth up to Jerusalem and cleanseth the Temple from defilement.*

Well indeed might Jesus stigmatize the chief priests of the Temple as hypocrites; for while these men were sticklers for such minor details of purification as the cleansing of cup and platter, they sanctioned, for the sake of gain derived from the rents of cattle-pens and shops, and from the sale of pigeons, the scandalous desecration of God's House by the filth and traffic of the great annual fair. This, though held certainly in the outer, or Court of the Heathen, to which all had access, must nevertheless, by its accompanying sights and noise and evil odours, have caused unseemly interruption and distraction to those worshippers who were intent upon the solemn services of the adjacent sanctuary. The reform inaugurated by Jesus on this occasion seems to have had certain definite, though but transient, results. Rules of almost unnecessary strictness were formulated and for a time enforced; but long-established custom, convenience, and greed, speedily combined to make such rules a dead letter, and, as we learn from the subsequent narrative, the condition of matters was within three years as bad as ever.

21. S. John iii. 1–5.—*Nicodemus, a Ruler of the Jews, cometh to Jesus by night to be further informed concerning his doctrine.*

It is frequently recorded that Jesus, for the sake of privacy and retirement, chose rather to spend the hours of rest in the open air, than in the comparative publicity and in the stifling atmosphere of an Eastern dwelling-room. We are justified, therefore, in preferring the housetop to the guest-chamber in endeavouring to visualize the secret interview which took place when " Nicodemus, a ruler of the Jews, came to Jesus by night."

22. S. John iv. 3–10.—*Journeying northward through Samaria, Jesus resteth by Jacob's Well, and revealeth himself to a woman of the country.*

Jacob's Well, which is situated about a mile from Shechem, is of great depth, and the consequent labour of drawing water has to a certain extent been reduced by constructing the mouth of the well in what is now an underground chamber, but which at a former period was probably an open area, to which access was obtained by a flight of steps. The slopes of Mount Gerizim are dimly discernible in the picture, shimmering in the dust-haze of the enervating sirocco.

23. S. Luke iv. 16–30.—*His teaching is rejected with fury by his own townsfolk of Nazareth, and he himself is thrust forth from the Synagogue and from the City.*

Drawings for the interior here represented were taken from the Synagogue of the Sephardim Jews, the oldest in Jerusalem. It shows the characteristic features of such places of worship; the central rostrum, occupied by the elders and the ruler of the Synagogue, and from the front of which the lessons for the day, with their *Midrash* or commentary, are read—the ruler's permission being granted—by anyone who may intimate a wish to officiate in this capacity. The latticed gallery conceals from view the women of the congregation.

24. S. Mark i. 21, 22 ; 32–34.—*The sabbath being ended, the people of Capernaum bring unto him many afflicted with divers diseases, and he healeth them.*

Nothing, save weed-grown ruins, marks the site of the once prosperous Capernaum, and the street in this picture, as well as other scenes laid in the same city, were therefore studied in Jaffa, also a seaport, and not otherwise dissimilar in situation.

NOTES ON PICTURES

25. S. MARK iv. 1–9.—*Because of the pressure of the multitude, Jesus seateth himself in Peter's fishing-boat, and teacheth the people many things by parables.*

Such beauty as the Sea of Galilee may be said to possess is attributable, not to the physical features of the landscape, which are tame and uninteresting, nor even to its local colouring, but to the ever-varying play of atmospheric effects. Full daylight does not display Gennesaret to advantage, whereas pearly dawn and sunrise, the flush of sunset upon the bare hills of Bashan, and moonlight, seen over the quivering waters of the lake, reveal scenes of loveliness which linger in the memory, and which owe their charm, partly it may be to association of ideas, but not a little at the same time to natural effect.

26. S. LUKE v. 4–7.—*The preaching ended, Jesus commandeth Simon Peter to let down his net in deep water, which being done, a great multitude of fishes is enclosed.*

The evidence of ancient monuments, and comparison of modern habits and customs with those incidentally recorded in the pages of Scripture, together with the proverbial conservatism and hatred of change which seems to be characteristic of all Eastern nations, warrant the assumption that the general features of daily life in Palestine have undergone little change since the days of Abraham; and the Levantine fishing-boat of to-day probably differs in no essential respect from those in which Jesus sat and taught, and in which he voyaged to and fro upon the Sea of Galilee.

27. S. LUKE v. 27, 28.—*Passing the Receipt of Custom, Jesus commandeth Matthew, the Publican, to follow him.*

The receipt of custom, which odious occupation Matthew quitted with alacrity at the summons of Jesus, doubtless refers to the "octroi" duty levied at the gates upon all goods brought into the city. The water-gate, leading from the harbour, is therefore selected for illustration.

28. S. LUKE vi. 12–23.—*Jesus goeth up into a mountain apart, whither he is followed by the multitudes and his disciples. From these he selecteth twelve to be his apostles, and he teacheth them.*

A visit to the "Horns of Hattîn" is convincing, if not of the accuracy of the tradition that this is the Mount of the Beatitudes, at least of the singular suitability of the place for the purpose it is said to have fulfilled. It lies at the head of the "Valley of Doves," a cleft in the hills which affords easy access to the summit from the neighbouring cities on the borders of the sea. Capernaum is in sight, not far from the place where the Jordan enters the lake, winding from its sources at the foot of Hermon, whose snow-capped ridge is visible thirty miles distant on the northern horizon. A few miles nearer, the roofs of Bethsaida are seen amidst the refreshing greenery of surrounding gardens and palm trees, and Magdala is close at hand at the foot of the valley. The summit of the hill is a small plain a few acres in extent, with a rocky "horn" or rising ground at either end, whence the voice of a preacher would readily be audible to the multitudes congregated on the lower level.

29.   S. MATT. viii. 1–4.—*The Sermon ended, he cometh down from the mountain and, meeting a leper, he cleanseth him.*

Lepers in Palestine are not so much in evidence as was the case in former days. For their own sake as well as for the public safety, these poor wretches are now confined in hospitals, but here and there a few are still to be seen sitting by the wayside begging, and uttering their piteous wail as they exhibit to the passer-by the ravages of their terrible disease.

30.   S. MATT. viii. 5–13.—*As Jesus entereth into Capernaum, there cometh to him a centurion, who beseecheth him on behalf of his servant stricken with palsy.*

Travellers will recognise in this scene the Square of the Fountain at Jaffa. The ancient pillars still surrounding the well in the form of an octagon, used to support a stone-built dome, which has been recently removed.

31.   S. LUKE vii. 11–16.—*At the entering in of a City called Nain, he raiseth from the dead a young man, the only son of his mother, and she was a widow.*

Nain is situated on the slope of a hill, misnamed "the Lesser Hermon," which forms the northern extremity of the ridge of Gilboa, and overlooks the Plain of Esdraelon, and Nazareth, from which it is distant about six miles. The ceremonial observed on the occasion of a funeral, such as is here referred to, obtains to-day as in Biblical times. The corpse, swathed in linen grave-clothes, the head being bound about with a napkin, is borne on an open bier to the place of interment. In a small community, the greater part of the population show their sympathy with the grief of more immediate friends and relations by following the body to the grave, while even the poorest would feel it a disgrace, did they not provide at least two hired mourners and two flute-players to lead the procession.

32.   S. LUKE vii. 36–50.—*At the house of Simon the Pharisee, he rejecteth not the love and service of a sinful woman, but rather forgiveth her.*

Either at Nain, or somewhere in the neighbourhood, Jesus accepts the hospitality patronisingly offered by a wealthy Pharisee to the new prophet. That an outcast woman should obtain access to the divan of a personage of austere religiosity may seem strange, although it is quite in accordance with Eastern custom, which does not refuse admittance to this semi-public part of the establishment, even to the most wretched and degraded, whose very touch

b

would be deemed a pollution. At this period of history, Jews of the better class had adopted the Roman custom of reclining at meals; poorer folk retaining the ancient oriental habit, which still obtains, of sitting upon the mat-covered floor around a low central table a few inches in height.

33. S. LUKE viii. 22–25.—*Crossing the Sea of Galilee with his disciples, Jesus stilleth a tempest which had arisen.*

Such a tempest as is here described is no unusual occurrence on the Sea of Galilee, the peculiar depression of whose surface, and the resultant and rapid evaporation, explain the exceptional suddenness and violence of the storms which sweep down upon the lake from the cooler uplands of Gadara and Naphtali, and from Lebanon.

34. S. LUKE viii. 26–35.—*And in the country of the Gadarenes he is met by a demoniac from whom he casteth out a legion of devils.*

Calm succeeds to tempest. Dawn breaks upon a scene of unruffled peace, upon the boat rocking at anchor close to the shore, where the fishermen have lighted a fire of driftwood and oleander stems to dry their clothes and cook their morning meal. Jesus retires apart to renew, in rest and communion with God, the physical and spiritual force expended in the conflict of the previous night. Suddenly from one of the tombs which honeycomb the face of the adjacent cliff, rushes forth a raving, naked maniac, demon-tortured and bleeding from self-inflicted wounds. With half-articulate cries he falls upon his knees, and the frenzied passions that rage within his breast prove obedient as the elements, to the words of power, " Peace, be still."

35. S. MARK ii. 1–12.—*Returning to Capernaum, a paralytic man, because of the press, is let down through a roof at Jesus' feet.*

The difficulty of fully understanding the passage in St. Mark's Gospel, which forms the subject of this picture, disappears on examining the extremely primitive construction of the roofs of many oriental houses. A fire in the town of Tiberias provided the artist with the unexpected opportunity of witnessing the actual breaking-up of a roof; this, for lack of water, being resorted to as a means of smothering the conflagration. The roof, to which access was obtained, as usual, by an outside stair, consisted of a few beams inserted in the outer walls, upon which branches of trees and palm-leaves were roughly laid; the final covering of a few inches of beaten earth providing scant root-hold for that " grass upon the housetops which withereth before it groweth up."

36. S. MARK v. 22–34.—*On the way to the house of Jairus, whose little daughter lieth sick, he healeth a woman in the crowd, and commendeth her faith.*

The buttresses and arches which span the narrow street, the overhanging latticed windows, and the tiny shops, are characteristic of a western Asiatic city; while the vaulted corn market to the right suggests the adaptation for the present subject of the " Suk-el-Bizâr " of Jerusalem.

ILLUSTRATING THE LIFE OF JESUS

37. S. MARK V. 35–43.—*Arrived at the house of Jairus he findeth the child dead and raiseth her.*

The maid has "fallen asleep" upon the mattress or quilt which, laid upon the floor, and without other preparation, forms the customary Eastern bed.

38. S. JOHN V. 2–9.—*Jesus findeth an infirm man at the Pool of Bethesda waiting to be healed by the troubling of the water; he biddeth him rise and walk.*

A visit to the medicinal hot baths of Tiberias suggested to the artist the use of similar architectural construction in endeavouring to realise the five-porched Pool of Bethesda. The "troubling" of the water, which gave rise to the tradition of angelic visitation (omitted in the Revised Version), was probably due to the intermittent nature of the spring; thus resembling the periodic ebb and flow of that known as "St. Mary's Well" in the valley of the Kidron; if, indeed, the latter may not have been the fountain-head of the pool in question.

39. S. MARK vi. 31–44.—*Jesus, seeing the multitude, is moved by compassion, and miraculously feedeth them.*

Six miles across the lake from Capernaum is the little Plain of Batiha, bordered to the north by the marshes through which Jordan enters the sea, and backed by hills, the lower slopes of which, in the month Nisan, are clothed with refreshing verdure and wild flowers. Here was wrought the mighty miracle by which Jesus satisfied the hunger of a vast multitude; and here, as elsewhere, were doubtless to be found some who were stirred less by thankfulness for benefits received, than by envy at the supposed better fortune of their neighbours.

40. S. MARK vi. 45–52.—*Jesus, walking upon the sea, overtaketh his disciples.*

Urgently as his human nature needed rest and refreshment, Jesus worked no miracle to secure it; nor did he even take advantage of the solitude obtained after sending the multitudes away to their homes, and his disciples to Bethsaida. After a few hours spent not in sleep but in prayer, once more his miraculous power was exerted in love and mercy. He walked upon the sea, overtaking his disciples, so that no time should be lost in hastening to the relief of the wretched and distressed, who eagerly awaited his return to the western shore.

41. S. MATT. xv. 21–28.—*He testeth the faith of a Syro-Phœnician woman who cometh to him on behalf of her daughter.*

The picture illustrates the scenery and gardens in the neighbourhood of Beyrout, which lies on the coast at the foot of Lebanon and within the Syro-Phœnician border.

NOTES ON PICTURES

42. S. MATT. xvi. 13–20.—*Jesus asketh his disciples whom the people say that he, the Son of Man is—he is refreshed in spirit by Peter's confession that he is the Christ.*

The site of Cæsarea Philippi is one of the loveliest spots in Northern Palestine. On ground carpeted with an infinite variety of wild flowers, the traveller rests in the grateful shade of oak and mulberry, olive and fig tree. The sound of many waters is heard on all sides as they hasten from the adjacent slopes of Hermon to join the head waters of Jordan, bursting in strength from a cavern at the foot of a mighty cliff. Hither, with his handful of followers, came Jesus, weary and in deep depression of spirit, a fugitive from his own people, who had finally rejected him; and here, in reply to his searching and anxious enquiry, "Whom say ye that I am?" he received from Simon Peter the memorable confession, "Thou art the Christ, the Son of the living God."

43. S. MATT. xvii. 1–8.—*Jesus goeth up into a mountain with three of his disciples, and is transfigured before them.*

From the days of St. Jerome, when pilgrims first began the attempt to identify sites hallowed by sacred events, Mount Tabor has, until recent years, been regarded as the Mount of the Transfiguration. But closer examination of the text and comparison of dates, and the fact that Tabor itself was at that time the site of a fortified town containing a Roman garrison, combine in this instance to discredit tradition. One of the spurs of Hermon must therefore be the alternative and more probable scene of the Transfiguration; the seclusion of this district of mountain, valley, and woodland providing opportunity for contemplation, and preparation for the end which was now imminent, "the decease which Jesus was to accomplish at Jerusalem."

44. S. LUKE ix. 37–42.—*Coming down from the mountain Jesus healeth a boy from whom his disciples had failed to cast out a devil.*

The picture gives a fair representation of the outskirts of a village in Northern Palestine, with its sordid, untidy, mud-built houses, on the roofs of which are seen the reed booths or *Succôth*, occupied by the inhabitants during the oppressive heats of summer. The snow-capped ridge of Hermon is indicated in the distance.

45. S. JOHN viii. 3–11.—*Jesus being asked to judge a woman taken in adultery, bids those who are without sin cast the first stone at her.*

The scene is represented as taking place in one of the great cloisters or porticoes which surrounded the Temple courts, and which, like the Forum of Rome and "Paul's Wall" in Elizabethan London, served the purpose of a public promenade and place of meeting. These porticoes were of magnificent construction and proportions, the Stoa Basilica alone, upon the south side, with its quadruple colonnade of one hundred and sixty-two pillars, covering an area greater than that of York Cathedral. The Eastern Cloister, known as "Solomon's Porch," was probably so-called as having been erected upon the site of a similar construction in the first Temple.

46. S. LUKE xvii. 11–19.—*Jesus, having cleansed ten lepers, is grieved that but one returneth to give thanks, and he a stranger.*

The town of Cana in Galilee, with its background of low hills, as seen from the Nazareth Road, supplies a landscape setting for this picture.

47. S. LUKE x. 38–42.—*He resteth at Bethany in the house of his friends, Martha, Mary, and Lazarus.*

Bethany is situated on the southern slope of the Mount of Olives, about two miles from Jerusalem. The house of his friends, Martha, Mary, and Lazarus, the only place which, during the latter part of his ministry, Jesus could call a home, was probably that of people in easy circumstances, and as such it is here represented. In the vineyards of Palestine the vine is cultivated bushlike on the ground; but in gardens, the plant is occasionally trained erect, as in Europe, or, as in the present instance, for the purposes of shade, upon a pergola.

48. S. MARK x. 13–16.—*He blesseth little children, and chideth those who would keep them from him.*

In the Talmud it is stated that, according to pious custom, parents brought their little children to the synagogue that they might receive the benefit of the prayers and blessings of the elders. Rabbis also, of recognised sanctity, were frequently appealed to in a like manner; and his fame as a prophet and benefactor having preceded him into Peræa, infants were now brought to Jesus, that he might lay his hands upon them in supplication and blessing. The architectural setting of the picture is adapted from that of a small square near the Damascus Gate of Jerusalem.

49. S. JOHN xi. 1, 3–6, 14, 15, 38–44.—*He raiseth Lazarus from the dead.*

The picture illustrates a form of rock-cut tomb which, though not so common as others in the neighbourhood of Jerusalem, is nevertheless selected as being in accordance with the description of what took place in the present instance. It is obviously the type of tomb which is referred to on a subsequent occasion, and explains the meaning of "the stone rolled away from the sepulchre." The entrance of the tomb is at the bottom of a flight of steps, and is covered by a disc-shaped stone, like a mill-stone, which can be rolled back into a slot cut in the rock for its reception. (The kneeling man in the background has apparently just performed this duty.) The entrance is closed by rolling the stone forward, dropping a small block behind it to prevent its recession, and finally by covering the before-mentioned slot with a slab, which, being cemented down, the tomb is "sealed."

NOTES ON PICTURES

50. S. Luke xix. 1–10.—*Jesus summoneth Zacchæus the publican to entertain him at his house.*

The sycomore tree referred to in the text is a species of fig, bearing small, coarse fruit, which is used as food only in cases of necessity. Although occasionally of great size, the tree is easily climbed, as the trunk is short, and the branches are numerous and wide-spreading.

51. S. Mark x. 46–52.—*Leaving Jericho, he restoreth sight to blind Bartimæus who sat by the wayside begging.*

The site of Jericho is still an oasis in the surrounding desert, but neither its fertility nor its dimensions bear comparison with those which it attained in former days; and hardly a trace remains of the celebrated groves of balsam, spice, and fruit-bearing trees, and the palms which earned for Jericho the title of "The City of Palm-trees," and which made its neighbouring plain the garden of Palestine—the " divine district," as Josephus calls it. This fertility was owing entirely to skilful irrigation, traces of no less than twelve aqueducts having been discovered by Col. Conder. No class of sufferers more frequently claimed and obtained from Jesus the exercise of his compassion and healing power than that represented by blind Bartimæus. The malady of blindness is grievously common in Palestine, the proportion of those thus afflicted being one in every hundred of the population, whereas in Europe the proportion is only one in a thousand.

52. S. Matt. xxi. 1–11.—*Jesus, riding on the foal of an ass, entereth Jerusalem, the multitudes shouting, " Hosanna to the Son of David."*

Had Jesus omitted the command to bring its mother along with the colt, upon which he elected to ride, his disciples would probably have brought her as a matter of course. It is the custom of the country; and as journeys are accomplished at a walking pace, mares and she-asses are frequently accompanied by their foals. It may be noted that in this picture one of the gates of Hebron does duty for that through which Jesus makes his triumphal entry into Jerusalem; the former being suggestive of far greater antiquity than any which are to be found at the present day in Jerusalem itself.

53. S. Luke xix. 47, 48 ; xx. 1–8.—*Jesus thereafter teaching daily in the Temple, the priests demand of him by what authority he doeth those things.*

The occasion on which Jesus encountered for the last time the opposition of his priestly enemies to his teaching, and when, in the presence of the assembled multitudes, he exposed and denounced their hypocrisy, is supposed to take place in one of the great outer courts of the Temple, the buildings of which, although begun forty-six years previously, were at this time still unfinished, and were indeed never fully completed in accordance with their original design.

54. S. LUKE xxi. 37.—*At night he leaveth the city and abideth in the mount, called the Mount of Olives.*

As we ascend towards sunset the slopes of Olivet, and pause to gaze on the scene beneath, the panorama of the city presented to view is in its leading features essentially similar to that upon which the eyes of Jesus rested, when "at night he went out, and abode in the mount that is called the Mount of Olives." Yonder stands a temple within that sacred enclosure which, for well-nigh three thousand years, save for the period during which "the abomination of desolation spoken of by Daniel the prophet stood in the Holy Place," has been dedicated to the worship of Jehovah. The citadel of Jerusalem breaks the skyline where stood the tower of Hippicus, and to the left, against the setting sun, the cypresses in a monastery garden mark the spot once covered by the gardens of the Palace of Herod. Siloam stands as of old on the hither side, overlooking the valleys of Hinnom and Kidron; while to-day, as in former times, the oliveyards beneath and the trees around, might well give the name which it bears to the hill on which we stand.

55. S. JOHN xiii. 1–10.—*Jesus, with the Twelve, partaketh of the Passover feast in an upper Chamber. He teacheth humility by washing the disciples' feet.*

A dwelling-house, claiming to be one of the most ancient in Jerusalem, supplied materials for the study of the "large upper room," represented in this and in other pictures. The general features of the chamber, with its arched ceiling and flattened dome, its *leewans* and the entrance-passage of coloured stones, where guests leave their foot-gear before stepping upon the mat-covered floor of the room, may, for reasons adduced elsewhere, be accepted as typical of similar apartments of the period under consideration.

56. S. JOHN xiii. 21–30—S. MARK xiv. 22–26.—*Thereafter he breaketh bread, and giveth them the cup, commanding them to do this in remembrance of him.*

In note No. 32 comment has already been made upon the custom prevailing at this time of reclining at meat. We are aware, from other sources of information, that in partaking of the Passover, the attitude of standing had, as a point of ritual, long been abandoned in favour of the recumbent posture, and this is directly evidenced by the words of the text (John xiii. 23 and 25), which are only compatible with the supposition that on the present occasion the guest-chamber was furnished with triclinia in the usual manner. Authorities differ as to which was regarded as the "highest seat," some maintaining that this was the outermost place on the right-hand couch; others, again, preferring the arrangement followed in the picture, where Jesus occupies the centre of the central triclinium.

NOTES ON PICTURES

57. S. MATT. xxvi. 36–46. — *Jesus then proceedeth to Gethsemane with his disciples, where, going apart from them, he prayeth in agony of spirit.*

As the word Gethsemane means the "oil-press," the "Garden" was in all probability an oliveyard, whose actual site, though it cannot be determined with certainty, must have been in the immediate vicinity at least of the spot which age-long tradition indicates as the scene of the Agony. The great age of the trees in this enclosure has been urged in favour of the tradition, but it is fatal to their claim as witnesses, that Titus is known to have cut down, for military purposes, all the trees in the neighbourhood of the besieged city.

58. S. JOHN xviii. 3–6—S. MATT. xxvi. 48–56.—*Judas having received a band of men and officers from the priests followeth to Gethsemane, and there betrayeth Jesus with a kiss.*

Cunningly conceived indeed was that signal of the kiss; for in the very act of betrayal, Judas thus covered his own treachery; and, had the plot failed, it would even have appeared as if, when "all the disciples forsook him and fled," Judas alone had courage, in the hour of danger, to stand by and openly to acknowledge Jesus as his Master.

59. S. MATT. xxvi. 57–66.—*Jesus, brought before Caiaphas and the Council, is accused of blasphemy and condemned.*

The outward ceremonial of the hastily-convoked and irregular tribunal before which Jesus underwent the mockery of a trial, was similar to that of the ancient Sanhedrim. The members sat on a semi-circular divan, the president in the centre, and a scribe at each extremity, who recorded the evidence and the decisions of the court. It may be noted, that while laws had been carefully formulated for the conduct of such trials, almost every one of them was flagrantly violated on the present occasion in order to ensure a pre-arranged condemnation. For example, these rules provided that witnesses should be summoned, and that an advocate should plead on behalf of the accused; and they forbade that criminal trials should be conducted at night, that condemnation should be pronounced on the day of trial or on a holy day; and, if the crime were capital, that execution should follow on the day of sentence.

60. S. MATT. xxvi. 69–74—S. LUKE xxii. 61, 62.—*Peter, having before cock crow three times denied his Master, repents as Jesus turns and looks upon him.*

In the East, the houses of the great and official residences usually consist of a group of separate yet connected buildings, surrounding a quadrangular paved court planted with trees and flowering shrubs, and furnished in the centre with an open cistern or fountain. Such was probably the construction of the Palace of the High Priest, and, apparently, this open court, across which Jesus would be conducted to or from the hall of trial, was the place where bitterness was added to his sorrow in hearing himself denied by his friend—that man who had been the first to profess belief in his Messiahship, and who, but a few brief hours before, had stoutly sworn to stand by him, even unto death.

61. S. John xviii. 28, 29—S. Luke xxiii. 2.—*Early in the morning Jesus is brought to Pilate, the Governor, and vehemently accused before him.*

Priding themselves upon their strict administration of justice, the Romans not infrequently erected their tribunals in the open air, by the city gate, in the market-place or theatre, or even by the roadside, in order that all might have the opportunity of seeing and hearing. The design of Herod's magnificent palace, now the official residence of Pilate, evidently made permanent provision for this method of judicial procedure, the "Gabbatha" being a tesselated pavement in front of the Judgment Hall, to which access was obtained by a flight of steps. In the centre of this pavement was a slightly-raised platform, upon which was placed the curule chair of the procurator, with seats to right and left for the assessors; other officers of the court occupying benches on the lower level.

62. S. John xviii. 33-38.—*Pilate privately examineth Jesus regarding his claims to kingship.*

If Herod's palace was built according to the customary Roman method, the private examination of Jesus would naturally be conducted either in the library, or in Pilate's business room—apartments which usually occupied positions on opposite sides of a short passage leading from the further extremity of the spacious atrium to the inner halls and chambers of the palace.

63. S. Luke xxiii. 4-11.—*Pilate then learning that Jesus belongeth to another jurisdiction, sendeth him to Herod.*

While in residence at Jerusalem, Herod Antipas occupied the ancient palace of the Hasmonæan kings, situated on the western hill, and not far from that built by Herod the Great. A weak, cruel sensualist, Antipas, like other princelings of his family, affected the dress and manners and the refined luxury of the Greeks. Blasé and wearied doubtless with the monotonous pleasures of his dissolute Court, he welcomed the excitement promised by the appearance of Jesus at his judgment-seat, anticipating that the prisoner would thankfully purchase his life at the cost of amusing the Tetrarch and his courtiers by some display of the magical power with the possession of which rumour had credited him.

64. S. Luke xxiii. 13-19—S. John xix. 1.—*Herod sendeth him back to Pilate, who, though unconvinced of his guilt, delivereth him to be scourged.*

In endeavouring to apprehend, however imperfectly, the sufferings endured by Jesus during this terrible day, there may be a tendency to underestimate the significance of one detail which is only incidentally mentioned

c

by the Evangelists, viz., the punishment of scourging. But this was nevertheless so barbarously cruel, that the mind recoils in horror from the effort to realise the awful agony which it entailed. Bound in a crouching attitude to the pillar of torment, the quivering flesh lacerated by the fragments of bone and metal intertwisted with the thongs, few of its victims, save such as were in perfect physical health, were able to survive the infliction of the scourge, but perished either then and there, or shortly afterwards, from nervous shock or from mortification of the wounds. Yet it was a punishment so common, such an everyday occurrence, that the scourging of one more malefactor—Jesus by name—the justice or injustice of whose sentence they neither knew nor cared to know, would be regarded with utter indifference by the brutal soldiery charged with its infliction.

65.   S. MATT. xxvii. 27-30.—*Jesus, arrayed in mock state, is brutally entreated by the Roman soldiers.*

Had it been possible to add a pang to the suffering already endured, this must surely have been effected by the foul jests and ribald mockery which Jesus was now called upon to endure at the hands of the ruffians of the barrack-room. The lust of cruelty, delight in inflicting and witnessing torture, marks the lowest depth of human depravity; and to sorrow of heart beyond what we can comprehend, to physical suffering as great as any which mortal man can endure and live, was now added the humiliation of being the object of sport and derision to the dregs of mankind. For these men were not even Romans, save in name; the ranks of the imperial armies called upon for foreign service being mainly recruited from the scum of the population of tributary provinces.

66.   S. JOHN xix. 4-6—S. MATT. xxvii. 23-26.—*Pilate declaring himself guiltless of his blood, nevertheless yieldeth Jesus to be crucified.*

Once more the scene is Gabbatha; and Jesus, his lacerated shoulders covered with a cast-off soldier's cloak of scarlet, and wearing a crown of thorns, is exposed to the gaze of the rabble of Jerusalem, who now surged and thronged in the courtyard of the palace. Pilate vainly hoped that the sight of the sufferings the prisoner had already endured might satisfy the fury of his enemies; but the relentless hatred of the priests was voiced through the insensate yells of the ignorant and bloodthirsty mob, and their final argument was cunningly directed to the point of least resistance. Pilate's sense of justice yielded to that of self-interest. "He released unto them one who, for sedition and murder, was cast into prison, whom they had desired; but he delivered Jesus to their will."

67.   S. LUKE xxiii. 26-31.—*Jesus, sinking under the weight of his cross, biddeth the women who compassionate him to weep not for him but for themselves.*

Needless to say, the route followed by the actual "Via Dolorosa" is lost beyond recovery, its very direction being entirely dependent upon that of Calvary, the site of which has for long been a matter of controversy. In any case the veritable Path of Sorrow lies concealed beneath a mass of débris, the ruins of the ancient city upon which modern Jerusalem is built. The street in the picture does not form part of the traditional route; it is the " Street of the Shoemakers," a coincidence which recalls the mediæval legend of " The Wandering Jew," who, it may be remembered, was a follower of this craft.

68. S. LUKE xxiii. 32–35.—*Coming to a place called Calvary, Jesus is there crucified and two others with him.*

In spite of all that has been spoken and written on the subject, the site of the " place called Golgotha " remains, as has been said, and must always remain, undecided. But to those who can maintain an open mind, unbiassed by sentimental associations, the weight of evidence bears heavily against the traditional Calvary (which shares with many other " sacred sites " the shelter of the Church of the Holy Sepulchre) and in favour of a little knoll overhanging the Grotto of Jeremiah, about an arrow-flight beyond the Damascus Gate of Jerusalem.

69. S. JOHN xix. 25–27.—*Jesus chargeth John with the care of his mother.*

Oft-repeated words are apt, for this very reason, to lose the force of their significance; and the Cross of Calvary has furnished so frequent a theme for Christian literature and Christian art, that it is by an effort only, which we do well to exert, that the anguish of that lingering death can even dimly be appreciated. The harrowing details have often been recounted, and it is sufficient here to state in brief, that it comprised, in one awful agony, well-nigh every pang which the human body can be called upon to suffer; withholding for long the boon of Death itself, and even the pitiful mercy of isolation. For that " lifting up," by which artists have striven to indicate the loneliness of Jesus, is not in accordance with the facts of the case. No timber in Palestine is of sufficient size to furnish crosses such as are generally represented, and we are forced instead to picture the patient sufferer during those weary fatal hours, as raised but slightly above the level of the ground, and literally face to face with his tormentors.

70. S. LUKE xxiii. 44–48.—*Jesus yieldeth up the Ghost, and the multitude return to their homes in fear of what they have seen.*

Of the various points of evidence which may be adduced in favour of the identity of the spot referred to in Note 68 with the Golgotha of the Gospels, one only need here be dwelt upon. " The place of a skull " is the interpretation of the Hebrew word as given in our Authorised Version, but according to the Revised Version "the place called ' The Skull ' " is the more accurate translation, and the singular suitability of this name to the hillock in question is obvious to anyone looking at it from the Mount of Olives; the caves and apertures in the face of the cliff beneath its rounded summit bearing a strange resemblance to the eye-sockets and nostrils of a human skull. The significance also of the words, "They that *passed by* railed on him," is at once apparent; as the knoll is in full view of passers-by to east and north, standing as it does at the junction of the high roads from Jericho and Damascus.

71.   S. LUKE xxiii. 50-56.—*Joseph of Arimathæa craveth the body of Jesus, and layeth it in his own new tomb.*

In a garden beneath this cliff there is a tomb bearing marked characteristics. The workmanship shows it to be Jewish and of the Herodian period, yet when first discovered there were traces of a cross painted upon the wall. Although there is room in the sepulchre for four loculi, one only of these has been completed, one only occupied. In digging near the foundations of a neighbouring monastery, a Christian grave was found bearing the remarkable words, "Laid near his Lord." We may never know the real meaning of these facts, but they are at least significant, and especially so in view of the cogent arguments which can be urged against the acceptance of the traditional site of the Holy Sepulchre.

72.   S. LUKE xxiii. 56; xxiv. 1-9.—*Early on the first day of the week come certain women to the sepulchre bringing spices. They see a vision of angels who declare that Jesus is risen from the dead.*

This and the following picture present the chief features of the rock-hewn tomb above referred to. It is about fifteen feet long by eleven feet wide, and eight feet in height, and it is divided transversely by a flattened arch supporting the roof. The single completed grave is formed by the erection on the floor-level of a limestone slab in notches cut in the rock for its support, thus forming, with the walls, a sort of built sarcophagus. An additional hollow, cut in the rock for the reception of the head, explains the meaning of "the napkin that was about his head" being "*in a place by itself.*" Sepulchres of this type are comparatively rare, and, providing as it does a minimum of accommodation for the labour expended on its construction, this new tomb must obviously have belonged to a man of wealth.

73.   S. JOHN xx. 3-10.—*Peter and John hasten to the sepulchre; they see and believe.*

The peculiar construction of the tomb furnishes an interesting commentary upon the text, of which this picture is an illustration. John is described as coming first to the sepulchre, "and he stooping down, and looking in, saw the linen clothes lying; yet went he not in." Why? Because, from his position at the entrance, he could perceive in the uncertain light the outline of the grave-clothes, and he hastily concluded from their undisturbed appearance that the body of his Master must still be there. Peter, with characteristic impulsiveness, entered in, and announced the startling discovery that the body of Jesus was indeed removed. "Then went in also that other disciple," and further examination revealed the well-nigh incredible fact that the grave-clothes and the head-napkin had simply *fallen together* in a manner only compatible with the supposition that they had not been unwound, but that in some mysterious way the body of the Lord Jesus had actually risen through the cerements of the tomb, leaving not a fold disturbed. As yet the two disciples had not grasped the meaning of their Master's words that he should rise again, nor of the prophetic utterance of David; but now, they "saw and believed."

74. S. JOHN xx. 11–18.—*Jesus revealeth himself to Mary Magdalene.*

It would appear that Mary Magdalene was one of the little company of faithful women who came very early in the morning to the sepulchre, but that she had hastened back to the city before the angelic revelation to her companions. Once more bending her steps in sorrow to the empty grave, to Mary, loving greatly because greatly forgiven, was vouchsafed the privilege of first beholding her risen Lord and Master—the same, yet wondrously changed, so that now, as on subsequent occasions when Jesus appeared to his disciples and "their eyes were holden that they should not know him," it was not by outward form and aspect, but by words of love and tenderness such as he alone could utter, that his identity was revealed. Although the external aspect of the sepulchre bears little resemblance to that which it presented in former times, the rock-cut grooves which still remain, render it abundantly evident that the entrance with its rolling stone, and the method by which the latter was "sealed," were such as have already been described in No. 49.

75. S. LUKE xxiv. 13–27.—*He draweth nigh to two disciples journeying to Emmaus, and proveth to them from the scriptures that Jesus is very Christ.*

Efforts to identify Emmaus with any existing village within the prescribed radius of "threescore furlongs" from Jerusalem have proved unsuccessful, and its actual locality is still a matter of controversy, in spite of the assistance which might have been anticipated from the name itself, the word Emmaus signifying "warm springs." Consensus of opinion, however, is in favour of some situation in the hill-country to the north-west of the city, possibly El-Kubébeh.

76. S. LUKE xxiv. 28–34.—*Jesus appeareth to Simon Peter.*

Beyond the simple statement that "he was seen of Cephas," nothing is recorded regarding the appearance of Jesus to his sinning and repentant disciple, although, if we accept the sequence of events in the order in which they are narrated, it may safely be supposed that this took place after night-fall. But where nothing is known, conjecture is justifiable, and we may think of Peter as shrinking from the society of his comrades, unable to rest, and wandering he knows not whither, in the silent, moon-lit streets. Chance leads him to the door of the house of Caiaphas, and there, on the scene of his lost opportunity, he realises the presence of his risen Lord, and receives the gracious assurance of forgiveness.

77. S. JOHN xx. 19, 20 ; 24–29.—*Again he appeareth to his disciples, and chideth Thomas for his unbelief.*

Five times during that memorable Easter Day did Jesus manifest himself to his followers, and it was not until the eighth day at even, that the sixth appearance is recorded as having taken place; this time for the special purpose of confirming the belief of one of the eleven who still doubted. Ten manifestations in all are specifically mentioned, but it would appear (Acts i. 3) that Jesus also revealed himself to his chosen apostles on many other occasions, speaking of the things pertaining to the building up of that Church, of which he was himself at once the Foundation and the Corner-stone.

78. S. JOHN xxi. 1–14.—*Once more Jesus sheweth himself to Peter and others by the Sea of Galilee.*

Next in order of the recorded appearances is that by the Sea of Galilee, whither the disciples had returned to await the promised meeting with their Master, the seven who were fishermen resuming meanwhile their former occupation. Disheartened and weary with a fruitless night's toil, they were returning homewards at dawn, when they perceived in the dim light the figure of one who had seemingly come down to the shore to buy their fish; and supposing from his words that he had noticed indications of a shoal, they readily followed his directions, laying out the net in the manner still in use upon the lake. The success of the cast at once suggested its true cause, and Peter, standing naked in the boat after swimming round with the net to "ring" the fish, paused but a moment to gird on his short, striped abba, and once more leapt into the sea, eager to verify the glad surmise that the stranger was none other than their Master himself. The background of the picture is the shore of the lake to the north of Magdala with the Wady Hammâm and Kurn Hattîn in the distance.

79. S. LUKE xxiv. 50, 51—ACTS i. 10, 11.—*Jesus, his work accomplished, ascendeth up into Heaven.*

"And he led them out as far as to Bethany," passing through the streets of the city, thronged with busy crowds, who knew not that Jesus of Nazareth passed by. Over the ridge of Olivet there is a path leading to Bethany, and following this the traveller reaches a secluded spot on the farther slope of the hill, and within sight of the home that Jesus had known and loved; and he pauses in reverence, for these silent stones may have witnessed the crowning scene of the world's Redemption—Jesus, Son of God and Son of Man, received up into Heaven, a cloud of adoring angels concealing from mortal gaze his entrance through the everlasting doors into the Presence of the Father.

80. S. MATT. xviii. 20; xxviii. 20.—*But according to his promise he is ever present with those who worship him.*

Yet this is not the close of the Great Story, and the painter's work is incomplete unless he endeavours to visualise the Truth that, as the Master has promised, his presence and his blessing are with his faithful worshippers even unto the end of the world. The picture represents no special people or period or ritual, and the Byzantine architecture most fitly symbolises that One, Universal, and Apostolic Church, of which Jesus Christ is the Founder and the Head.

PRINTED IN GREAT BRITAIN BY
EYRE AND SPOTTISWOODE, LTD.,
HIS MAJESTY'S PRINTERS, LONDON